CHINA AND NEW ZEALAND:
A THRIVING RELATIONSHIP THIRTY YEARS ON

CHINA AND NEW ZEALAND:
A THRIVING RELATIONSHIP
THIRTY YEARS ON

Edited by James Kember and Paul Clark

New Zealand Asia Institute
The University of Auckland

Unless otherwise stated, the unit of currency quoted is the New Zealand dollar.

The New Zealand Asia Institute acknowledges the assistance of the Ministry of Foreign Affairs and Trade in the publication of this book.

New Zealand Asia Institute
Te Roopu Aotearoa Ahia
58 Symonds St
The University of Auckland
P O Box 92 019
Auckland
New Zealand

www.auckland.ac.nz/nzai

Copyright 2003 ©New Zealand Asia Institute

National Library of New Zealand Cataloguing-in-Publication Data
China and New Zealand: a thriving relationship thirty years / edited by James Kember and Paul Clark.
ISBN 0-473-09527-0
1. New Zealand—Relations—China. 2 China—Relations—New Zealand.
I. Kember, James, 1950– II. Clark, Paul, 1949– III. New Zealand Asia Institute (University of Auckland). IV. Title.
327.93051—dc 21

All rights reserved. Without limiting the rights under copyright reserved above, no part of this publication may be reproduced, stored in or introduced into a retrieval system, or transmitted, in any form or by any means (electronic, mechanical, photocopying, recording or otherwise), without the prior written permission of both the copyright owner and the above publisher of this book.

Cover and text designed by Egan-Reid Limited
Typeset by Egan-Reid Ltd, www.egan-reid.com
Printed in New Zealand

Contents

Contributors	7
Introduction James Kember	13
Thirtieth Anniversary Reflections Bryce Harland	19
Three Decades of Diplomatic Relations: Expectations and Outcomes Michael Green	27
Still Floating: No Longer Sojourners, but Transnationals Manying Ip	37
The Social Dimension: New Zealanders in China Matthew Dalzell	47
The Bilateral Economic Relationship and the Regional Setting Robert Scollay	61
New Zealand Business in China Alastair MacCormick	73
Relationship Dynamics and Strategic Calculus: A Chinese Perspective Yongjin Zhang	87
Shaping Our Future Relationship Rt. Hon. Helen Clark	99
Afterword: The Next Thirty Years Paul Clark	113

Prime Minister Helen Clark speaking to the New Zealand Asia Institute on 13 November 2002 [*Photograph: Godfrey Boehnke*]

Contributors

Rt. Hon. Helen Clark has been Prime Minister of New Zealand since November 1999 and is also Minister of Arts, Culture and Heritage, and Minister in charge of the New Zealand Security Intelligence Service. A graduate of The University of Auckland (MA (Hons) 1974), she taught at the university from 1973 to 1975 and again from 1977 until her election to Parliament in 1981. During her parliamentary career, she has chaired the Foreign Affairs & Defence and Disarmament & Arms Control Select Committees, and she also held a number of ministerial portfolios during the Labour administration of 1987–1990. She was awarded the Danish Peace Foundation's Annual Peace Prize in 1986 for promoting international peace and disarmament. In 1993, Helen Clark became Leader of the Opposition, a position she held until the return of the Labour Party to government in 1999.

Paul Clark is Professor of Chinese in the School of Asian Studies, The University of Auckland and Director of the China Studies Centre, New Zealand Asia Institute. An Auckland graduate in History, in October 1974 he was one of the first three students to go to China to study under official exchange auspices. He studied for two years at the Beijing Languages Institute and Peking University. A PhD in History and East Asian Languages at Harvard University followed. After ten years at the East-West Center in Honolulu, Clark returned to New Zealand to his present position in 1993. A specialist on Chinese film and popular culture, he is currently engaged in research on culture during the Chinese Cultural Revolution (1966–1976).

Matthew Dalzell has been actively involved in New Zealand-China relations, as a historian and official, since 1989. His monograph *New Zealanders in Republican China, 1912–49* was published by the New Zealand Asia Institute in 1994, and he has been an affiliate of the Institute since it was founded. He is a graduate of the University of Auckland (BA Asian History, English; MA History) and Beijing Normal University (Modern Standard Chinese), and lived for four years in Beijing 1996–1999. He joined the Ministry of Foreign Affairs and Trade in 1993, and is currently seconded to the New Zealand Agency for International Development. The views outlined in his paper are personal, and are not a statement of New Zealand Government policy.

Michael Green is Deputy Secretary for Political and Security Affairs in the Ministry of Foreign Affairs and Trade. He was previously New Zealand Ambassador to Indonesia (1997–2001). A career diplomat since 1970, he has also served in Thailand (1972–1975), at the New Zealand Mission to the United Nations in New York (1978–80), and in China (1981–1982). In Wellington his assignments have included periods as Director of the Ministry's South & Southeast Asian Division and North Asian Division, and he was for six years (1988–1994) Director of the External Assessments Bureau in the Department of the Prime Minister and Cabinet.

Bryce Harland was a member of the New Zealand Foreign Service from 1953 to 1991. After serving in Singapore, Bangkok, New York (UN) and Washington, he became New Zealand's first ambassador to China in 1973. Returning to Wellington in 1976, he became an Assistant Secretary in the Ministry of Foreign Affairs and Trade, and later Director of External Aid. In 1982 he returned to New York as New Zealand's Permanent Representative to the United Nations. In 1985 he was appointed High Commissioner for New Zealand in London – the first professional diplomat to hold the job. He retired from the Foreign Service at the end of his term in London in 1991. He then held Visiting Fellowships at All Souls College, Oxford and Wolfson College,

Cambridge, and continued living in England until 1996. Upon returning to Wellington, he was appointed Director of the New Zealand Institute of International Affairs and held the position until 2002. His major publications include On our Own: New Zealand in the Emerging Tripolar World (1992), Asia: What Next? (1992), and Collision Course: America and East Asia in the Past and the Future (1996).

Manying Ip is Associate Professor in the School of Asian Studies and Associate Dean of Postgraduate Studies within the Faculty of Arts of The University of Auckland. She teaches the Masters papers on Chinese New Zealanders and on Chinese Translation as well as undergraduate papers on Classical Poetry and Rethinking China. Her recent publications include Re-Examining Chinese Trans-nationalism in Australia—New Zealand (ed.) published by Australian National University Press; Unfolding History, Evolving Identity: the Chinese in New Zealand by the Auckland University Press; "Chinese Female Migration: From Exclusion to Transnationalism" in Lyndon Fraser & Katie Pickles ed. Shifting Centres: Women and Migration in New Zealand History published by Otago University Press; "Trans-Tasman Parallels: As seen through a century of Chinese Migration, 1901–2001" in Arthur Grimes, Lydia Wevers & Ginny Sullivan eds, States of Mind: Australia and New Zealand 1901–2001 published by the Institute of Policy Studies of Victoria University of Wellington; "Maori-Chinese Encounters: Indigenous-immigrant interaction in New Zealand" in Asian Pacific Review; "Chinese Political Participation in New Zealand: the role of Taiwanese Migrants" in Essays on Ethnic Chinese Abroad, Volume II, Academia Sinica, Taipei; and "Chinese Business Immigrants to New Zealand: Transnationals or Failed Investors?" in Re-examining Chinese Transnationalism in Australia-New Zealand. She has been a highly respected advocate for the Chinese communities. She was awarded the Suffrage Centennial Medal in 1993, and the ONZM (Officer of New Zealand Order of Merit) in 1996.

James Kember has been Director of the New Zealand Asia Institute since 2001. A graduate of Victoria University of Wellington and of the Institute of Commonwealth Studies at the University of London, where he completed a PhD on India's external relations prior to independence, he joined The University of Auckland from a foreign service career of over twenty years that included postings in Beijing, twice in Hong Kong (most recently as Consul-General 1998–2001), at the United Nations in New York, Nouméa and Rarotonga, and as Private Secretary to the Minister of Foreign Affairs and Trade (1994–1997). Since 2001, he has also been a member of the board of the New Zealand Committee of the Pacific Economic Cooperation Council.

Alastair MacCormick, formerly Deputy Vice-Chancellor (Academic) of The University of Auckland, is an Emeritus Professor of the University. He is currently a director and consultant with experience in the business, education, research, government and not-for-profit sectors. As an academic and consultant, for over thirty years he has worked at the interfaces between university education and research, business and government. His posts include Chairman of the Board of Richina Pacific Limited, a publicly-listed New Zealand corporation with international operations; Director of the commercial construction firm Mainzeal Corporation; Director of Shanghai Richina Leather Corporation, one of the largest finished leather tanneries in China; Director of Blue Zoo International in Beijing; Chairman of Avant Consulting Group Ltd, of NETdelivery Australasia Limited, and of AeroQual Limited, a venture producing new sensors for the measurement of physical air quality. His long-term interest in Asia-Pacific affairs is also manifested by his former membership of the New Zealand Committee of the Pacific Economic Co-operation Council. He was also New Zealand Coordinator for the APEC Human Resource Development Working Group for four years after its founding. These activities enabled Dr MacCormick to play a significant role in the establishment at The University of Auckland of the New Zealand Asia Institute, the APEC Study Centre for New Zealand and the Department of International Business within the School of Business and Economics, all of which support the extensive network of active relationships the University now enjoys throughout Asia and the Pacific.

Robert Scollay is Associate Professor of Economics at The University of Auckland. He joined the Economics Department in 1979 and was appointed director of the New Zealand APEC Study Centre in 1995. His recent research and publications have focused on issues relating to regional trade agreements and regional integration, especially in the Asia-Pacific region, and to multilateral liberalisation and globalisation. With Susan St John of the Economics Department he has also co-authored a widely-used series of first-year economics textbooks. He is currently coordinator of the PECC Trade Forum, a network of trade experts from countries around the Pacific Rim. He has undertaken consultancies on trade issues for a number of international organisations, as well as for agencies of the New Zealand and Australian governments.

Yongjin Zhang is Associate Professor and Head of the School of Asian Studies of The University of Auckland. He won the British International Studies Association (BISA) prize (1991) for the best article published in *Review of International Studies*. Dr Zhang has taught at Oxford and at the Institute of International Politics, Beijing, China. From 1999 to 2001 he was Fellow at the Department of International Relations, Research School of Pacific and Asian Studies, The Australian National University. He has been honorary Senior Fellow of the Institute of Asia-Pacific Studies of the Chinese Academy of Social Sciences since 1996. Dr. Zhang has written *China in the International System, 1918–1920* (1991) and *China in International Society since 1949: Alienation and Beyond* (1998). He has also edited (with Rouben Azizian) *Ethnic Challenges Beyond Borders: The Chinese and Russian Perspectives of the Central Asian Conundrum* (1998). These three books are published in St. Antony's-Macmillan Series by Macmillan in London. His more recent publications include *Power and Responsibility in Chinese Foreign Policy* (co-edited with Greg Austin, Asia Pacific Press, 2001), "System, Empire and State in Chinese International Relations", in *Review of International Studies* (2001), "The English School" in China: A Travelogue of Ideas and Their Diffusion" in *European Journal of International Relations* (2003); and *China's Emerging Global Businesses: Political Economy and Institutional Investigations* (Palgrave, 2003).

NEW ZEALAND ASIA INSTITUTE

Introduction

James Kember

December 2002 marked thirty years of diplomatic relations between New Zealand and the People's Republic of China. In the nature of anniversaries, it seemed appropriate to reflect not only on the past three decades, rapidly developing and bourgeoning as the relationship has been, but also on some of the earlier linkages, extending back into the nineteenth century. It was in this thirtieth year of formal relations with China that the state offered its apology for the discrimination levelled in earlier decades against Chinese migrants. But this anniversary also offered an opportunity to look ahead from the prism of late 2002 at how one of New Zealand's patently key bilateral relationships might develop in the years to come.

The Institute itself has marked earlier anniversaries. In 1997, for the twenty-fifth, it organised commemorative conferences in Beijing and Shanghai. On this occasion, it was decided to hold a public mid-winter lecture series and, in keeping with the Institute's mandate, to produce a publication that, like the lectures themselves, would take stock of a relationship at this particular waypoint.

The bilateral relationship has of course been reviewed previously. Among key publications have been the proceedings of the 21st Otago Foreign Policy School (published as Ann Trotter (ed.), *New Zealand and China*, University of Otago, 1986), Lindsay Watt's *New Zealand and China Towards 2000* (Institute of Policy Studies, Victoria University of Wellington, 1994) and John McKinnon's chapter "Breaking the Mould: New Zealand's Relations with China", in *New Zealand in World Affairs, Vol III, 1972–1990* (edited by Bruce Brown, 1999, for the New Zealand Institute of International Affairs). Victoria University also published *New Zealand and China: Present and Future* in 1996, a series of contributions that were edited by Tim Beal and Yongjin Zhang.

The most recent of these publications is now four years old; and there have been a number of significant developments since then, including China's entry to the World Trade Organisation. On 18 December 2002, at a 30th anniversary commemoration in Auckland, former WTO Director-General Rt Hon Mike Moore said that for him, getting China into the Organisation was more important than achieving a new trade round – though it was of course of some satisfaction that both were achieved during his tenure. China, he recalled, has always been the world's largest economy – except over part of the last two hundred years. He suggested that no serious New Zealand exporter should be in business without at least an annual visit to China.

Several major visits in recent years have demonstrated the strength of New Zealand's relations with China, including the bilateral visit by President Jiang Zemin after the 1999 Auckland APEC meeting. The last few years have also witnessed rapid growth in Chinese students and migrants to this country. This has had a considerable impact not only on the provision of education services but also on the national economy more generally; and it also fuelled a debate during and since the time of the General Election in July 2002 about immigration and language requirements for entry. These developments brought China sharply into focus, because of the weight of numbers of migrants as well as students.

INTRODUCTION

The University of Auckland acknowledges the importance of Asia in a variety of ways. Apart from the work of this Institute in promoting research and debate, its School of Asian Studies is now the largest such in the country with over 2500 students and a wide range of courses, including a full range on China and the Chinese language. The university participated in the May 2002 visit to China by the Minister of Education, Hon Trevor Mallard, with calls on government and education institutions in Beijing and Shanghai. As the Deputy Vice-Chancellor, Dr Raewyn Dalziel commented when introducing the Prime Minister for her address in the lecture series:

> It would be fair to say that this university is keenly aware of playing its part in building stronger – and mutually-reinforcing – people-to-people links with China. It can, and will, do this through its own, internationally-recognised, teaching and research strengths.

In particular, Professor Dalziel noted the strength of the School of Asian Studies and the comprehensive Asia-related research of staff not only in that School but also in many other faculties including the sciences, engineering, information systems and international business. In respect of China, she also noted the important academic and student linkages established with leading Chinese universities including Peking, Tsinghua and Fudan.

In designing the series of lectures that gave rise to the papers that follow, Paul Clark and I were keen to identify contributors from this university, government and business who had had some particular direct connection with China. As the bionotes and the papers themselves demonstrate, we were fortunate in this respect. We were also grateful to the Prime Minister for agreeing to give the concluding lecture and offer a prognosis on the future of the relationship. Having noted the growing importance of China internationally as well as the strength of the current bilateral relationship, whatever the occasional short-term pressure points, the Prime Minister concludes that a new era in New Zealand's relations with China has begun. The basis, she notes, is there for New Zealand to share in China's future, and in that of its people.

In his remarks, reflecting on a very long association with the People's Republic, New Zealand's first Ambassador to Beijing, Bryce Harland, suggests there is good reason to hope that New Zealand's relations with China will develop as well in the coming half of this century as they did over the course of recent decades. As others note later, the future success of New Zealand's bilateral relations has to be seen very much in the key context of Sino-United States relations.

The papers that follow attest to a relationship that has grown exponentially and – as Foreign Affairs Deputy Secretary Michael Green notes – well beyond the cautious expectations of 1972. Many of the contributors can point to examples of China's opening up to the world. My own first visit to Beijing, in 1978, involved an 11-hour journey not from distant New Zealand but just from Hong Kong, and included two trains, one plane and having to cross the border on foot. The reverse journey was much the same, but with an obligatory overnight stay in Guangzhou as well. Coca-Cola (and all that that implied) had yet to arrive. The major trading point was the biannual 'Canton Trade Fair' in Guangzhou.

The advances in the economic and business relationships are outlined by Emeritus Professor Alastair MacCormick and Associate Professor Robert Scollay. They offer an insightful account of the changing dynamics around doing business in China, and the likely impact on these bilateral relationships of China's accession to the World Trade Organisation.

Against evidence of a rapidly-expanding economy, Alastair MacCormick sounds a note of caution to those potential exporters hoping to gain from increased consumer spending power. He points to high rates of savings, the likelihood of ploughing income into private homes, and a fierce loyalty to local brands as factors that need to be incorporated in any calculations about projected sales in China of foreign-made products. The experiences of various New Zealand enterprises in recent years, as he sets these out, are particularly instructive.

Robert Scollay suggests that because China and New Zealand are essentially not competitors in terms of their principal exports, New Zealand does not stand to be adversely affected by China's WTO entry (as other major textile and clothing exporters could be). He cautions nevertheless that New Zealand, in order to obtain the gains from China's rapid economic growth, should now be looking to diversify its range of exports. China, as he reminds us, will itself be the main beneficiary of its WTO accession.

Robert Scollay also addresses the various debates and negotiations now in train over regional trading arrangements in East Asia. He notes the potential for New Zealand to be excluded from new arrangements and makes the point that China does not stand to be adversely affected by New Zealand and Australian inclusion in new configurations that centre on the principal northeast Asian economies. Indeed, he says, China offers New Zealand considerable potential as an ally in pursuing such a goal. The challenge is there for the taking.

The importance of China's WTO entry is also addressed by Michael Green who notes that this development, apart from changing the way of doing business with China, also heightens awareness in China's neighbours of the strategic implications of China's emerging economic power. He takes the view, however, that whatever the nature of bilateral difficulties that might arise in the trade area, the greatest challenges to the relationship in the short term will come in the area of people-to-people links, including issues of migration and student entry.

On those people-to-people linkages both Associate Professor Manying Ip and Matthew Dalzell recall that contacts in both directions go back many years, Chinese first coming to New Zealand in the 1860s and New Zealanders working in China from the early decades of the twentieth century. Dr Ip asks whether Chinese are these days any more considered equal citizens than they were in the past when the measure of a 'good Chinese' was how 'English' he had managed to become. The debate as to whether migrants should assimilate and become 'New Zealanders', however that might be defined, far from being quiescent seems rather to have been rekindled of late. Dr Ip cautions that to ignore Asia, and Chinese people, would not only be for New Zealand to under-utilise talent, but would also blind the nation to its own real identity. Both she and Matthew Dalzell point to the way residents of China and New Zealand are now moving continually in both directions, exemplifying the transnational nature of today's world.

Some of the strategic aspects of the relationship, and the broader international context, are set out in the paper by Associate Professor Yongjin Zhang. It is based on, but takes further, an address he had prepared for the lecture series but was unable to deliver. Writing from what he describes as "the Chinese perspective" he notes that the past three decades have been each quite distinct, leading, one by one, to a higher state in this bilateral relationship.

Paul Clark, in an afterword written for this publication, takes this assertion one step further, in laying down some of the steps for maximising advantage. His call to increase the exposure of New Zealanders to China, to make greater strides in the teaching of Chinese history and language in schools, and to establish a New Zealand-China Foundation are all worth serious and early consideration. At the same time, we in the Institute have been suggesting that it is also time for China, for its part, to consider the establishment of a China Foundation. Such an organisation could, like its counterparts in Japan and the Republic of Korea, provide a focal point for counterpart activities on spreading understanding of Chinese political, cultural and economic imperatives into those countries like New Zealand whose future is so intimately bound up with that of the People's Republic.

This series – and certainly this publication – would not have been possible without the support of the Ministry of Foreign Affairs and Trade and its staff in Wellington and Beijing. Apart from contributing speakers, the Ministry has also kindly made a grant towards the costs of this publication. Thanks, too, to the contributors first for participating in the lecture series and then having the patience to turn their speaking notes into papers for publication, and to Emeritus Professor Nicholas Tarling for his editorial assistance. We hope this collection of papers will spur further discussion on and understanding of relations between New Zealand and China.

Thirtieth Anniversary Reflections

Bryce Harland

After thirty years of increasingly close contact and cooperation, it takes an effort to remember that until 1972 New Zealand had no official relations with China. A number of New Zealanders had lived and worked in China at various times, some for long periods, as traders, teachers or missionaries, but there had never been any official New Zealand representation. Then in 1950 war broke out in the Korean peninsula: New Zealand became involved, and so did China – on opposite sides. The two countries were cut off from each other for more than twenty years, and even pitted against each other at the United Nations – in the offshore islands crisis of 1955, as well as in the long-drawn out struggle over Chinese representation.

In this period Rewi Alley played an important part in keeping up unofficial contacts. He kept in touch with his family and friends in New Zealand, and his work in China attracted widespread interest and sympathy. But most New Zealanders still knew little about China, and had only vague impressions of the country and its people.

Things began to change after President Nixon went to China in 1972. He met Chairman Mao Zedong and Premier Zhou Enlai, and they found that Americans and Chinese could work together. Their meetings opened the way for other countries to widen their contacts with China as well. New Zealand did not seize the opportunity immediately: it took general elections and changes of government in both Australia and New Zealand to overcome domestic resistance to breaking long-standing ties with Taipei. But in December 1972 both of the new governments formally recognised the People's Republic of China, and established diplomatic relations with Beijing.

One officer in the then Ministry of Foreign Affairs had been trained in 1950s to speak the Chinese language. He died prematurely in 1972, just before relations were established. As head of the Asia Division in the Ministry, I was asked to accompany the Associate Minister, Joe Walding, on the first official New Zealand mission to China. We arrived in Beijing at the end of March 1973, in the Chinese spring. We had several meetings with the Deputy Foreign Minister, and then one with Premier Zhou himself. The Ministers quickly agreed to give substance to the new relationship by exchanging embassies, trade missions and students. After our return to Wellington, I was appointed the first New Zealand ambassador to China. Our embassy in Beijing opened in June, and I presented my credentials in September.

Rewi had already been living in China for over forty years, and he had travelled widely there. He welcomed us warmly, and helped us to understand what was happening around us. The Cultural Revolution was still going on, seven years after it had been launched by Mao to revitalise the Communist Party. Rewi had suffered at the hands of the Red Guards, and did not admire them. But he pointed out that 'the good old boys' were coming to the fore again, and the country was beginning to settle down. We shared this perception with the stream of visitors we were beginning to get from New Zealand, which included the then leader of the National Party, John Marshall. He went home to find that he had been ousted by Robert Muldoon, who proved to be more interested in China than Marshall. Meantime we had been working with the Chinese authorities to broaden the range of contacts between our two countries. Exchanges of sports teams, acrobats, scientists, potters and musicians were filling out the relationship: we even had a visit from the National Youth Orchestra, who were warmly welcomed by their counterparts in China, as well as by the New Zealanders there.

It is sometimes said that the Kirk Government recognised Beijing to promote New Zealand's trade with China. That is not correct: Kirk explained his action by saying that, in an increasingly multipolar world, New Zealand had to be able to talk to the Chinese and the Russians as well as the Americans and the Europeans. But the action taken for political reasons did have economic benefits. Before recognition our exports to China had fallen to just over $1 million. By 1975 they had risen to $25 million, and they went on growing. China now takes nearly one billion dollars' worth of New Zealand products each year, and Hong Kong as much again.

After China I returned to Wellington, and did not get back to Beijing until 1978. A brief visit then showed me that, after the death of Mao and the fall of the 'gang of four', the Cultural Revolution had at last come to an end, and Deng Xiaoping was opening China up to the world. My old Chinese teacher was delighted that his children would now be able to go to university. (One of them eventually came to live and work in New Zealand. He and his wife are both architects, and they contribute more than a little to our own society.) During the three years I was in New York as Permanent Representative to the United Nations (1982 to 1985) I saw many Chinese officials, including my old friend Zhang Wenjin (former Vice-Minister of Foreign Affairs and China's Ambassador to the United States 1982–1985), and sometimes worked closely with them.

Soon after David Lange became our Prime Minister in 1984, I was sent to London. There my interest in China was renewed by my very able Chinese counterpart, Ji Chaozhu (Ambassador to the United Kingdom 1987–1991), who had earlier been personal interpreter for both Mao and Zhou, as well as by several British diplomats who had served in Beijing, and by discussions on China at the Ditchley Park conference centre near Oxford. The Tiananmen incident in 1989 shocked us all, and made some wonder whether China had changed so much after all. My experience in China made me reluctant to draw any such conclusion. The sight of thousands of young people demonstrating in Tiananmen Square must have reminded some older people of the Red Guard marches which had begun the Cultural Revolution in the 1960s, and the anarchy that followed, and led them to accept the use of force, despite the inevitable effect on China's reputation abroad. My feeling that China was not going back to the days of Mao was borne out by Deng's reaffirmation of his policy of opening China up, and this gradually became accepted in the outside world. But it was not until I was able to go back to China in 1993 that I felt sure there was no turning back. Apart from its great monuments, like the Imperial Palace and the Temple of Heavenly Peace, Beijing was hardly recognisable. China was attracting foreign investment on a vast scale, and using it to good purpose. There were already new roads and buildings everywhere, and the roads were choked with cars, buses, and trucks, instead of with the bicycles which had been ubiquitous in the 1970s.

But the biggest change I saw was in the Chinese people. During the Cultural Revolution they were not allowed to talk to foreigners, and few had the courage to do so. By the 1990s they would talk about anything, including politics. They seemed to feel free, despite the well known restrictions on human rights. They were enjoying their new-found freedom to acquire skills, to get jobs, and to improve their living conditions. Later visits confirmed that the changes were still going on, and in the same direction. China was not yet a democracy, but it was clearly becoming a more open society, as well as a more prosperous one. Those leaders who were at the helm as the new millennium dawned are now retiring, but they committed their successors by undertaking to hold the Olympic Games in 2008, and by joining the World Trade Organisation.

China has not joined the WTO to please other countries, no matter how important they are. It has joined because its experience over the last 25 years has convinced the Chinese that trade liberalisation is the way to achieve and sustain fast economic growth and the reduction of poverty.

A recent Chinese visitor to Wellington pointed out that the impact of joining the WTO will be as great as that of Deng's decision to open the country up. Now China is at last in the WTO it will have to make another round of far-reaching changes in its economy and its society. Some of these changes will involve serious disruption and hardship. But educated Chinese know that those changes have to be made, not just to satisfy WTO requirements but to keep China moving towards prosperity. Having come so far, it cannot afford to stop: it's like riding a bike.

The change in China does not seem likely to stop. Something like half a million young Chinese are now studying abroad. Those who go home afterwards are not only better educated than their elders: they are more cosmopolitan in their outlook, more confident, and more nationalistic. They want China to catch up with the West, and play the prominent role it used to play in world affairs. They also want more say in the way China is governed – but not at the expense of China's national unity. To them, as to their elders, the reunification of China is a paramount goal – final proof that the century and a half of foreign domination has ended. Hong Kong has returned to the national fold, without losing its identity or its standard of living. Macao has returned too, after 500 years as a Portuguese colony. The remaining problem is Taiwan.

That island was part of China long before the Japanese forced the Chinese to give it up in 1895, and ran it as a colony for 50 years. When the Nationalist forces were decisively defeated by the Communists in 1949, many of them took refuge in Taiwan, and Chiang Kai-shek wanted to use it as a base from which to attack the mainland. After war broke out in Korea in 1950, the United States ordered its Seventh Fleet to patrol the Taiwan Strait to prevent either side from attacking the other. Under American guidance, and with American aid, the Nationalists built up a strong economy, which gave people in the island a higher standard of living than people on the mainland. Some of those on the island – especially those whose families had lived there for a long time – began to press their claim to independence from China, despite the fact that they shared the same language and culture. But businessmen in Taiwan saw the mainland in a different light. During the 1990s it became their second-largest market, after the United States. They invested heavily there too: Taiwan interests are said now to have over $100 billion invested on the mainland. Costs there are lower, so investment on the mainland is a way to increase competitiveness. They are now keen to establish direct sea and air links, particularly with Shanghai. Beijing continues to insist that Taiwan is part of China, and Taipei must accept the One China principle 'indefinitely'. Beijing is presumably hoping that pressure from businessmen will eventually bring about a change in Taipei's position. So far, there is no sign of this happening.

What can New Zealand do to help avert a conflict in the Taiwan Strait, and bring about a peaceful settlement? Not very much, but not nothing either. The position of the New Zealand Government remains as it was defined in December 1972 – we recognise the People's Republic as the sole legitimate Government of China, and acknowledge its position that Taiwan is part of China. That is also the position of most other governments, including the United States. It precludes any official link with the authorities in Taipei, but New Zealanders are free to have cultural and economic relations with people in Taiwan, and they do.

The main thing New Zealand can do to help bring about a peaceful settlement of the Taiwan problem is to stick firmly to our established position. We must avoid any action that might encourage either party to try to change the present position by force. Most of the time there is little we can do beyond that, but occasionally we do get a chance to do something useful. During the APEC Summit in Auckland in 1999 our Governor-General hosted a private meeting between the Chinese and American Presidents. That broke the deadlock caused by the bombing of the Chinese Embassy in Belgrade, and led to the reopening of negotiations on China's admission to the WTO. It was regarded by both parties as a helpful action on our part.

But we need to be careful. Because China has such a big population, and occupies such a central position in the Asia-Pacific region, the political stakes are always high. The history of the last couple of centuries shows that when things in China go wrong, they go very wrong, and cause untold human suffering. The Taiping rebellion, which followed the Opium War, is now estimated to have cost 50 million lives. So I at least am thankful that at present things seem to be going right. The Chinese economy is still growing fast, when some others are faltering. Since Deng Xiaoping took over the leadership in 1978, some hundreds of millions of people in China have escaped from poverty and found some hope of continuing improvement in their lives. Another change of leadership is underway, as Jiang Zemin and some of his closest associates reach the age limits they set down for themselves. This is a critical moment for the future of China, but so far there is no sign of serious instability, or of any sudden change of course. Relations with the United States under President George W. Bush have not always been smooth, but the terrorist attacks on the United States on 11 September 2001 led to some easing of the pressure on China.

Perhaps the most hopeful thing is that tensions between Beijing and Taipei have eased, as businessmen on both sides see advantage in working together. There is a large and growing community of Taiwan business people in and around Shanghai, which is becoming, once again, the economic centre of the Chinese-speaking world, without any dramatic change in political arrangements.

All this gives reason to hope that New Zealand's relations with China will develop as much in the next half century as they have in the last. As we commemorate the 30th anniversary of the establishment of diplomatic relations, we need to look forward as well as back. There are questions to consider about New Zealand: are we a bicultural society or a multicultural one? Do we still see New Zealand as a Western country, or as one that now belongs to the Asia-Pacific region? These questions are still subject to debate, though a consensus sometimes seems to be emerging. There are also questions about China: is it seeking to extend its influence in the region – to become again the Middle Kingdom – or is it merely trying to improve the living conditions of its people? These questions have serious implications for China and for New Zealand: they concern the whole region.

Perhaps the key issue for all of us is the relationship between China and the United States. Experience during the last 30 years shows that when they work together or in harmony we all benefit greatly. But experience also shows that the relationship is tense, dynamic and volatile. And New Zealand is ineluctably involved. The big question for us is whether we can live in peace and friendship with both the great powers in the Pacific, yet avoid being drawn into their rivalry, for it is obvious that if we have to take sides we can only lose. During the last three decades it has seemed at times that New Zealand was becoming a test-bed for China's relations with other countries. Is this still the case? Can we continue to cooperate with both America and China, and even at times help to ease the strains between them? Do we really have to choose between them, or can we continue being friends with both? That seems to be what most New Zealanders want: can that goal be achieved?

Three Decades of Diplomatic Relations: Expectations and Outcomes

Michael Green

This seminar series marks the thirtieth anniversary of the announcement on 22 December 1972 of the establishment of diplomatic relations between New Zealand and the People's Republic of China. In this paper, I want to consider three questions:

≈ what has been achieved in the past thirty years?

≈ is it what the New Zealand Government expected in 1972?

≈ what does the experience of the past three decades tell us about what may lie ahead?

New Zealand's decision to recognise the People's Republic was narrowly based on geopolitical considerations; economic and trade prospects played little part in the decision. People-to-people contacts on a significant scale were scarcely contemplated. Our government would have been prescient indeed had it anticipated the dynamism of today's

Chinese economy, the degree to which China's economy and society would be opened up to foreign influence and participation, or the level of bilateral interaction, governmental and non-governmental, that we now take for granted. In 1972 these things were hardly thinkable. China then was an insular society, bruised by the revolutionary excesses of its political elite. A foreign policy built around exporting revolution had made it an object of international suspicion, the more so as it stood outside virtually all of the multilateral institutions. Its isolation was reinforced by an autarkic economic philosophy which limited growth and development and opportunities for trade.

New Zealand opinion about China was considerably influenced by the Korean War, in which China fought on the opposite side, and by the perceptions of friendly governments in Southeast Asia which felt themselves under threat from Chinese Communist subversion. There was widespread sympathy in New Zealand for the government on Taiwan, which New Zealand recognised and whose right to represent China in the United Nations New Zealand had defended until the General Assembly voted to seat Beijing's representatives in 1971.

What motivated New Zealand decision-makers to recognise the People's Republic was an awareness of a shift in international alignments that made engagement with China both possible and desirable. They saw that China was adopting a less ideological foreign policy stance, and moving towards engagement with the established international system. Their formal justification for establishing diplomatic relations was a geopolitical assessment which concluded that New Zealand needed to follow a more self-reliant foreign policy. Prime Minister Norman Kirk made this explicit in a speech on the day the establishment of diplomatic relations was announced:

> There are now four great powers involved in the affairs of Asia and the Pacific – the United States, Japan, China, and the Soviet Union. Each is playing an active and independent role and each expects its friends to look after themselves more than in the past. The policies and activities of all four have an important bearing on developments throughout the region.

In this situation it is essential for a small country like New Zealand to be in a position to deal directly with all four powers. We must keep ourselves informed of what they are thinking and doing. Our national interests also require that we have the means of making our views known, and getting them heard, by the great powers. To do this we must have effective diplomatic representation in all four capitals. . .

China has now re-entered the mainstream of world affairs. It is playing an active part in the United Nations. In Asia and the Pacific its influence is great, and is bound to grow. It is logical and sensible for New Zealand to recognise the People's Republic of China and enter into normal relations with it.[1]

Judged against this objective, New Zealand's engagement with China has clearly been successful. From the earliest days of representation in each other's capital there have been worthwhile and sometimes robust explorations of international issues and respective national policies towards them. New Zealand has made its views known directly and had them heard at the highest levels in China. It helped in the beginning that China saw New Zealand as sharing China's hostility to Soviet expansionism. The overwhelming priority China assigned to this anti-Soviet foreign policy meant that several issues which New Zealand had assumed might be difficult to manage bilaterally – its membership of ANZUS and SEATO, for example – scarcely figured in the bilateral dialogue.

Today, with anti-Sovietism no longer relevant, exchanges of view continue through the respective embassies, through the high level visits that have become part of the fabric of the relationship, and through institutionalised frameworks for regular consultations between officials. These cover the whole spectrum of shared interests: trade and economic cooperation; disarmament and security; development assistance; human rights; regional cooperation; and the environment; as well as a wide range of specifically bilateral matters, often highly technical. In all these

---

[1] Norman Kirk, *New Zealand in the World of the 1970s*, Wellington, Ministry of Foreign Affairs, 1972, p. 5.

areas, the exchanges are no less wide-ranging or frank than those with New Zealand's other regular interlocutors.

That said, it is not easy to demonstrate that New Zealand's views have influenced Chinese policies. Even our early support for China's WTO membership, and the technical and other assistance we provided to help China's preparations for it, had only a marginal impact, as the basic decision to join had already been made in Beijing. And the real test of influence is not in issues on which the two governments held similar views, such as WTO entry or opposition to Soviet expansionism, but issues on which they did not agree, such as nuclear testing, or Chinese policies towards Taiwan and Tibet, or specific trade access problems. On these, it seems to me, China has behaved like any great power, in practice largely impervious to the opinions of others, whatever the formal willingness to hear them.

From today's vantage point a striking feature of Norman Kirk's 22 December speech is the absence of any reference to trade or economic benefits of establishing diplomatic relations: in the whole text he said only that economic and trading matters "are inseparably linked with foreign affairs". There were at that time a few vocal advocates of China trade possibilities, including business-people who had long engaged in it. But scepticism ran deep. This was reflected in a speech the year before by Kirk's predecessor, Keith Holyoake, who argued that China's emphasis on "self-sufficiency rather than the expansion of international trade" was a reason to be cautious: he pointed out that China's foreign trade was then only about double New Zealand's. He also questioned, on the basis of Chinese growth data since 1949, whether recently reported high growth rates in China could be sustained.[2]

But there was a fundamental misunderstanding of China's approach. For the Chinese, political relations were a pre-condition for everything else. Commercial contacts – and cultural ties – were not seen as things

---

[2] "New Zealand and China", *Foreign Affairs Review*, Wellington, May 1971, pp. 3–12. See also statement of 8 June 1971 in *Foreign Affairs Review*, Wellington, June 1971, pp. 64–65.

to be pursued for their own sake. They were an expression of, and a consequence of, the political relationship. Within the first year after the establishment of diplomatic relations the two Trade Ministers had exchanged visits and a bilateral trade agreement had been signed. This agreement conferred MFN status and set in place a formal mechanism, the Joint Trade Commission, to foster trade and to review progress on trade issues. Two-way trade then began to grow. In 1972 (June year) the total value was $11 million (of which $2.5 million was New Zealand exports); thirty years later (2002 June year) it was over $3 billion (of which $1. 4 billion was New Zealand exports).

Because expectations of trade and economic benefits were very modest in 1972, these figures should be cause for considerable satisfaction. Indeed, trade with China grew faster than that with New Zealand's other trading partners. China's share of New Zealand's total trade was less than half a percent in 1972, and now accounts for around five percent. And these are merchandise trade statistics, which take no account of the substantial sums New Zealand earns today from tourism and education. But China remains some way below the top tier of our trading partners, well behind the big four – the US, Australia, Japan and the EU – and New Zealand's percentage share of China's imports has remained pretty constant for almost a decade. The returns from investment flows in both directions have been patchy. We have done well in trade and economic relations but there is plenty of scope to do better.

The establishment of diplomatic relations also made possible the resumption of non-governmental links with the Chinese mainland that had withered after 1949 in the absence of formal inter-governmental ties. This did not happen quickly but the growth in scale and diversity of these connections – in business, education, tourism, sister-city relations, cultural exchanges, immigration, sport and professional or technical areas – is one of the great strengths of the relationship today. They seem set for further significant expansion. Of the bilateral interaction before 1949, only Christian missionary work has not resumed. As Matthew Dalzell shows, in the first half of the century it had been the channel through which a great many New Zealanders gained some knowledge of China, a partial understanding to be sure but a generally sympathetic one. I believe these positive impressions facilitated the revival of people-to-people contacts after 1972.

From this brief survey it would seem that New Zealand's 1972 assumptions about and expectations of the benefits of a relationship with China were too cautious and conservative. That is the wisdom of hindsight. Caution and conservatism were widespread long after New Zealand recognised China. An anecdote from my own experience may illustrate this point. I was Counsellor in the Embassy in Beijing in the early 1980s when the Chinese authorities announced the goal of quadrupling GDP by 2000. The broad assessment of the diplomatic community was that this was technically feasible but most unlikely to be achieved. In fact, the target was reached with some years to spare.

In retrospect, it is clear that this analysis was deficient in at least two important respects. Its assumptions were too static. It underestimated China's capacity to change and adapt as the policy of modernisation and opening up introduced new ideas, technologies and capital. It underestimated the impact of foreign travel and foreign educational opportunities on the thinking of Chinese decision-makers. It overlooked the evidence from other Asian economies that transformation can be very rapid, given appropriate policy settings and consistent implementation.

And a proper historical perspective was lacking. The frame of reference for judgements about what might be feasible was the Communist era. This was both too short and too turbulent to be useful in making projections for the next twenty years. We forgot that, except for the period beginning about 1890, China's economy has always been the world's biggest. There is now a pretty broad consensus that China will again become the world's largest economy within a few decades – perhaps as soon as 2015 or 2020; more likely a decade or two later.

That prospect makes China's entry into the WTO a seminal event. It signalled the international community's acknowledgement that China has arrived as a significant force in the world economy. It opened the way to managing the integration of the new economic giant by subjecting it to the same trade rules and disciplines as other economies. And, by no means least important, it formalised China's willingness to work within the rules-based international trading system. That does not mean that trade problems will disappear but it goes some way towards levelling the playing field between China and a small economy like New Zealand.

For some countries, reliance on the WTO is not enough. China's WTO entry has reinforced in China's neighbours an awareness of the strategic implications of China's emerging economic power. The recent burst of proposals for new regional co-operation arrangements – two initiatives by Japan's Prime Minister Koizumi, ASEAN Plus Three, the ASEAN/China Free Trade Arrangement, several proposed bilateral FTAs with China or Japan or Korea – are partly about positioning other economies to deal with a dominant Chinese economy; to benefit from it if at all possible, or to limit damage from it if not.

This may be symptomatic of deeper concerns. China's growing economic power, military modernisation, and increasing engagement in international issues and organisations imply greater Chinese political and strategic weight in the Asia-Pacific region and beyond. There is now a considerable literature debating the proposition that this development poses a threat to the established regional order, or to the interests of individual countries, and should be resisted. Even many who do not necessarily regard China's rise as threatening acknowledge that it could be destabilising, as other countries have to accommodate themselves to the reality of Chinese power. Bryce Harland wrote an excellent book about the potential for a collision between the United States and China, and he is not alone in seeing the risks. [3] If this critical relationship should deteriorate, New Zealand will face very difficult choices.

Even without a Sino-US collision, managing the China relationship will be a major challenge for New Zealand foreign policy in the next few decades. In facing this challenge we can draw some comfort from the fact that New Zealand has long been accustomed to working with, or in

---

[3] *Collision Course: America and East Asia in the Past and the Future*, Wellington, Institute of Policy Studies, and Singapore, Institute of Southeast Asian Studies, 1996.

the shadow of, a dominant power: first the UK; subsequently the US. We are familiar with managing an unequal relationship. But in dealing with a dominant China we will not have the framework of shared beliefs and assumptions that have helped us to work easily alongside the UK and US: a common language; a common heritage of law, history, and culture; democratic political systems; and a view of international law and multilateral institutions as regulators of the behaviour of states.

If the pace of change in China continues at anything like the rates of recent years, these differences may not have too much impact on doing business with China. Dealing with China will become more and more like dealing with other non-Western countries. But, as China becomes more influential, the demands of other countries for access to its decision-makers are growing. New Zealand will have to work hard to keep open the channels of communication built up over the first thirty years of diplomatic relations and to maintain constructive working contacts across the whole range of issues. In particular we will have to continue to be conscious of Chinese sensitivities in matters touching fundamental aspects of China's political order, such as the status of Taiwan or Tibet.

In the short to medium term it is not these fundamental issues that are likely to cause bilateral difficulties. Nor will it be trade policy disputes, though it is clear that monitoring China's implementation of its WTO undertakings, and negotiating solutions where problems arise, will loom large in the work of the Embassy in Beijing and of relevant departments in Wellington for some time to come. The greatest short-term challenges – the highest potential for relations to be soured – will arise in the area where bilateral links have grown most since 1972: people-to-people contacts.

The huge recent increases in Chinese student numbers, the growth of Chinese tourism, and the steady influx of Chinese immigrants are all creating risks of misunderstandings that could easily flow over into government to government relations. We saw this happen in the early 1990s when the collapse of several private English-language schools in New Zealand led to compensation claims that could only be resolved by government intervention. Official Chinese representations over recent thefts from Chinese tourists in Auckland have pointed up a new area of potential strain. There have been a variety of issues about resettlement of migrants that should lead us to look carefully at the way newcomers from China are received in this country.

Managing such problems is especially difficult because the New Zealand and Chinese governments have different views of the relationship between government and citizen and of the responsibilities and obligations each has in situations like these. But they require no less thought and care than the big political or security issues which may heighten tensions in our wider region. New Zealand will never be more than a bystander in developments between China and Taiwan but in these potentially awkward people-to-people matters it is a principal actor.

To sum up, I return to the three questions posed at the outset:

What has been achieved in the past thirty years?
A rounded and mature bilateral relationship has been achieved in thirty years of diplomatic relations with China, and New Zealand benefits greatly from it. Relations are not completely free of stresses and tensions but are closer and warmer than seemed possible thirty years ago.

Was it what the New Zealand Government expected in 1972?
This relationship is more diverse and more solidly grounded than anyone in the New Zealand Government expected in 1972. The range and depth of political contacts developed since then, and their number, have gone well beyond the most optimistic expectations. Trade and economic ties are far more important and dynamic than anyone anticipated then. In people-to-people contacts New Zealand expectations have been vastly exceeded.

What does the experience of the past three decades tell us about what may lie ahead?
The experience of the past thirty years confirms that prediction is fraught with risk. We have a much better base of information and experience

from which to think about and work with China than we had in 1972 but we still cannot be certain that New Zealand will be able to foresee, let alone devise strategies for dealing with, all the implications of China's re-emergence as a major power.

Still Floating: No Longer Sojourners, but Transnationals

Manying Ip

The people-to-people relationship is arguably the most potent and long-lasting in the history of New Zealand-China interaction. While it might sound mundane and nebulous, this relationship will have a determining role in shaping the future of other forms of bilateral links, political, economic, and cultural.

When asked about people-to-people relationships with the Chinese, the usual reaction of many mainstream New Zealanders will be: "They are our model minority!"[1] The usual clichés to describe Chinese people in New Zealand include: "[They have moved] from market gardeners to successful entrepreneurs" or "from undesirable aliens to valued citizens".[2] It is good for our national ego to feel that New Zealand's

---

[1] M. Hewitson, "From the Great Wall to Whangarei ; Chinese New Zealanders", *New Zealand Herald*, Auckland, 23 May 1996.

[2] R. McLeod, "China girl: the hard won victories of Mai Chen", *North and South*, August 1993, pp. 86–95.

egalitarianism and the open-mindedness shown towards ethnic minorities have enabled the Chinese, as the country's most longstanding non-Polynesian and non-Anglo migrants, to be successful.

However, when we listen to the utterances of populist politicians who trundled out Enoch Powell's long-discredited 'river of blood' theories; and observe how they play out blatantly anti-foreign messages when they supposedly 'only want to discuss immigration policy', this gives rise to Chinese people being seen as the 'eternal stranger' or/and 'necessary outsider' – the essential Other on whom every wrong thing could be conveniently blamed. Are the Chinese really considered as equal citizens of New Zealand? How integrated are they? And what role do they play?

In February 2002, when the Prime Minister publicly apologised to the community for the historical poll-tax and other discriminatory legislation inflicted on the Chinese, some Chinese actually criticised their leaders for asking for an apology, on the ground that they were very happy and contented. Some even went so far as to say that they considered the poll-tax quite justifiable. If anyone needs proof to show how the Chinese have been traumatised and stigmatised, this extreme diffidence and these over-conciliatory attitudes speak volumes.

To my mind, the people-to-people relationship between New Zealand and China could not really develop, let alone flourish, even after the recognition of 1972, because the Chinese were always 'on the back foot' and felt insecure as a stigmatised minority. Whether they can play a full positive role in future depends, therefore, on the collective will of all thinking New Zealanders, rather than mere government legislation, short-term economic considerations, or political expediency.

Historical People-to-People Relations
Although the early Chinese miners were invited by Dunedin to come and re-work the abandoned goldmines as early as the 1860s, they were excluded from the blueprint of the young colony, and later on the Dominion, and the young nation-state of New Zealand. They were merely tolerated because their labour was considered necessary. Their status was that of itinerant labourers, who should be repatriated as soon

as they were no longer useful. There was no intention whatsoever that the Chinese should be allowed to settle down to become a community in New Zealand.

That is why the Chinese were only allowed to come as single men, and the cries against miscegenation became very loud when they "consort[ed] with Irish women of the lowest type" or formed relationships with Maori women.[3]

No real people-to-people relationship to speak of existed in the period of discrimination, because the Chinese were never considered remotely equal, and were barred from citizenship (from 1908 to 1952) and even from long-term residency. They existed as an ethnic enclave on the fringe of respectable society. They were not considered assimilable and were never given a chance even to try to fit into the monocultural society around them. The most that they could hope for was not to offend, not to attract any attention, and not to arouse hostility. One can hardly call this a meaningful 'people-to-people' relationship.

It is therefore understandable that the standard New Zealand histories never mention a Chinese name. The *Dictionary of New Zealand Biography* published in recent years has tried to include some Chinese. Significantly, many were businessmen who could speak English, and acted as intermediaries: Chew Chong, Choie Sew Hoy, Ah Chee, Wong Doo – the group called 'useful Chinamen' by the ruling majority. The measure of a 'good Chinese' is how 'English' he was. When William Ah-Chee died in 1929, for example, *The Auckland Star* obituary referred to him as "Old Grammar School Boy, Prominent Businessman, Head of Fruit Firm. . . Although born of Chinese parents in Auckland, Mr Ah Chee was in thought, education, and habits an Englishman."[4]

---

[3] E & P. Beaglehole, *Some Modern Maoris*, Wellington, New Zealand Council for Educational Research, 1946, pp. 55–57, 321–323; T. Simpson, "The Yellow Yahoo", *Shame and Disgrace: A History of Lost Scandals in New Zealand*, Auckland, Penguin Books, 1992, pp. 194–221.

[4] M. Ip, *Dragons on the Long White Cloud: the making of Chinese New Zealanders*, Auckland, Tandem Press, 1996, pp. 43–44.

It was an unequal and unnatural relationship that confirmed the second-class status of the Chinese. The interactions most probably also misled mainstream New Zealanders into thinking that they were indeed generous, kind, and superior.

Even those who had close contact with the Chinese considered them a second-class race full of vice. Alexander Don, the missioner who spent decades working amongst the Chinese goldmines in Otago, harboured great resentment and prejudice against them. Katherine Mansfield who grew up in Wellington in the 1900s wrote about the Chinese in the most derogatory terms. Her impressions of the Chinese as disease-ridden, dirty, often insane and totally alien[5] probably reflect accurately the feelings of mainstream Pakeha of her times.

Model Minority Period (including post-1972 diplomatic recognition)

At the end of World War II, the Chinese community transformed itself from a 'broken-stem' bachelor society into one of real families. This big step forward was made more by accident than by design. Asia remained on the fringe of New Zealand imagination, and scant interest was shown in the Chinese people, who were numerically small and so low-profile and humble as to be almost invisible. The exclusion of the Chinese from mainstream Pakeha circles was considered quite normal. For example, Chinese New Zealanders served in both the First and Second World Wars. In spite of the close comradeship that existed within the armed services, the Chinese never joined the RSA, never marched on ANZAC Day, never partook of their rightful place in the sun. Apparently they were never invited to mainstream functions and celebrations.[6]

---

[5] See, e.g., "Ole Underwood" and "The Wind Blows" in Antony Alpers (ed.), *The Stories of Katherine Mansfield*, Auckland, OUP, 1984, pp. 131–133, 191–194.

[6] In 1995, this author helped to curate an exhibition on Chinese war service in New Zealand and conducted extensive interviews among the surviving veterans. The then RSA chairman was also interviewed.

No one asked why the Chinese did not join.

No matter how upbeat one wants to be, this is hardly evidence of an equal and positive people-to-people relationship:

> The monocultural society's more subtle and low-level discrimination virtually disempowered the community, forcing many of its most creative spirits into silent conformity and non-involvement... [Chinese New Zealanders] became a noncontesting group that gauged its success largely by how mainstream New Zealand rated them. [7]

Too often when the so-called Chinese success story is cited, the heavy price paid to earn this mainstream approval is forgotten. Rita Chung asserts that the apparent academic competence and single-minded devotion to studies mask great emotional stress: "Chinese youths may come to believe these labels and respond accordingly in some self-fulfilling prophecy."[8] Chung and Bevan Yee assert that the Chinese minority were powerless within the "hegemonic structure", and could only do their utmost to fulfill an "unspoken contract".[9] The contract between the dominant mainstream and the disadvantaged minority is that the latter should know exactly how far they could go. They are vulnerable, and their sense of non-belonging is manifested in being "extra good" and "trouble free".[10] Kirsten Wong speaks of the "pain of trying to cope with the stress of living up to a variety of often contradictory expectations: to be motivated but not assertive, to excel academically but not be competitive", to be successful and yet invisible – essentially, the anguish of trying to "know one's place."[11]

---

[7] Ip, *op.cit.*, p. 123.

[8] R. Chung et al., "From Undesirable Immigrant to Model Minority: The Success Story of Chinese in New Zealand", *Immigrants and Minorities*, Vol. 7, 1988, pp. 308–313.

[9] Ibid; B. Yee, "Enhancing Security: A Grounded Theory of Chinese Survival in New Zealand", *Education*, Christchurch, 2001, p. 250.

[10] Ibid.

[11] Ip, *op.cit.*, p. 124.

To have a significant ethnic minority feeling vulnerable and defining itself only negatively – by not arousing jealousy – is not conducive to the advancement of the nation.

Relations post-1990s

New Zealand's 1987 immigration policy changes, which opened its doors to 'quality migrants' with talent and capital (monetary, skills, and cultural) irrespective of country of origin, proved to have revolutionary results. It coincided with China's post-Cultural Revolution *gaige kaifeng* (Open Door) and Deng Xiaoping's pragmatic economic policies. China's initial worry about a brain drain has, in the recent decade, evolved into a more relaxed attitude of *laissez-faire*. The government allowed its people to acquire exit visas for purposes of family reunions, visits, study, and business. Self-funded overseas study became extremely common in China's big cities by the mid-1990s.

It is under this new set of circumstances that People's Republic of China migrants have been highest in number among the Asian immigrant cohorts from the late 1990s to the present. Many young Chinese professionals have come to New Zealand in search of better opportunities. They might qualify under family reunion or skilled migration. They usually would find it hard at first to get into the job market, and would seek re-training. Their number (around 9,000 in 2001), and their trend of trying to fit into the job market made them far more visible and potent a force than their Hong Kong or Taiwan counterparts.

The presence of this high-profile group has been challenging to New Zealand's policy makers. On a people-to-people level, the Chinese presence also required mainstream New Zealanders to re-define their racial attitudes. On the one hand, the new Chinese, together with other Asian communities, have given New Zealand a foretaste of what a vibrant and multicultural society could be like. The Asians are giving mainstream New Zealand advanced exposure to what this part of the world is really like – a world that had been shut out for more than a century and a half when mainstream New Zealanders looked more to 'mother England' than to their own geographical region.

The Chinese are also forcing mainstream New Zealanders to confront the reality that this is a country of an increasing mix of colours. In this part of the world where we are situated, the 'whiteness' has been fading fast. Ever since the new immigration policy of 1987, more Chinese people have been able to meet the stringent criteria and qualified to enter the country. Yet the less than enthusiastic reception they have met so far greatly hampered the development of strong people-to-people relationships. For a long time, they were commodified, and treated essentially as "walking money bags."[12] They were often not looked upon as would-be citizens, but rather tolerated just for the investment capital that they could bring.[13]

A worrying development in recent years is that the Chinese (and 'other Asians') have been treated as arch villains who showed no respect for New Zealand's environment, harvesting seafood indiscriminately. "Asians [are] raping New Zealand's coast", the news headlines screamed;[14] and the "Asian culture is to take everything."[15] Even worse, they allegedly had no understanding of the Treaty of Waitangi, our nation's founding document, and had no respect for the *tangata whenua*.

Conclusion

The chequered path of the New Zealand/China people-to-people relationship reflects the difficulty of New Zealand's road towards forming its own national identity. The inability to have positive

---

[12] L. Jones, "Too tough to make money in New Zealand, say business migrants", *New Zealand Herald*, 26 September 1991.

[13] M. Ip and W. Friesen, "The New Chinese Community in New Zealand: Local Outcomes of Transnationalism", *Asian and Pacific Migration Journal*, Vol. 10, 2, 2001, pp. 213–240.

[14] "Asians Rape Coast says Henare", *The Press*, Christchurch, 20 October 1994

[15] B. Reid, "Barren Times for Race Relations", *Time*, 17 May 1993, pp. 40–41.

relationships with Chinese is an indication of a basic problem of attitude and deficiency of knowledge. New Zealand has yet to come to terms with the reality of multiculturalism, largely because it has not yet freed itself from its own Euro-centric past.

The people-to-people relationship is moving fast, far outstripping its static self-image. New Zealand at present ranks fifth as China's preferred country of settlement, and fourth as a destination for its international students. New Chinese New Zealanders are adopting transnationalism, and blurring the line between 'Chinese in New Zealand' and 'New Zealanders in China.' For example, Hong Kong has the largest New Zealand community in Asia, boasting several thousand people. Already, the various New Zealand business and social associations in Hong Kong include large proportions of transnational new New Zealanders, formerly resident – and now back – in Hong Kong.

In my most recent field research conducted in Shanghai on 'returnees', most of them are New Zealanders working long-term in China, holding temporary work visas as 'foreign experts'. The new Chinese are still 'floating' but they are no longer sojourners lacking rights to stay in New Zealand. They are mostly New Zealand citizens or have rights of permanent residency. But at present the Chinese job market as well as the economic scene are much more attractive. They have become transnationals by choice.

These are interesting times, offering challenging phenomena for the analysis of social scientists. The best scenario involves Chinese New Zealanders participating fully and freely in all aspects of the nation's life, coming forward spontaneously in a totally uninhibited way. With their international outlook, linguistic skills, Asian market knowledge, and established networks, they can only be great assets to New Zealand. As I wrote previously: "When the Chinese, like all other New Zealanders, can function free from prejudice and stereotyping, they will do much to enhance the nation as a truly robust multi-ethnic modern society."[16]

New Zealand ignores Asia, and Chinese people, at its own peril – not

---

[16] Ip, op.cit., p. 162.

because China is strong, not just because of economic and trade implications, and not just because it under-utilises the talents of its Chinese citizens. More importantly, prejudice blinds the nation to its own real identity, and prevents it from moving forward constructively. If New Zealand should fail to engage its ethnic Chinese citizens fruitfully, it will be a sad case of *déjà vu*. More fundamentally, success in transcending the chequered people-to-people relationship with its longest-standing immigrant ethnic minority will signal a new stage of New Zealand's maturity. The social tolerance and self-confidence needed to engage positively with the new Chinese will be the hallmark of the best of New Zealand community development.

The Social Dimension: New Zealanders in China

Matthew Dalzell

As other contributors have also indicated, New Zealand and China have engaged and interacted in particular, and sometimes peculiar, ways over the last thirty years, from the political, economic, security, and trade perspectives. This paper endeavours to give a brief overview of one side of the social dimension of that contact, the people-to-people aspect of New Zealanders travelling, staying, living in China, complementing Manying Ip's paper about Chinese in New Zealand.

Given the changes over time, some questions worth exploring are "Where are we now on the growth curve?", "Where next?", and "What will be the main influences of growth or decline in the social dimension of the relationship in the medium term?"

The key to the two periods of growth in the social contacts, that is to say with significant numbers of New Zealanders going to China to live and work, 1912–1949, and 1972–present, are the frameworks which made that possible. Government agreements, which could be variously *permissive, protective,* or *facilitative,* opened the door. Faced with an open door, New Zealanders based their decision to walk through it on a combination of cultural factors, family ties, and trade and other opportunities. Many of these issues are common to the Republican period and to the period after 1972.

Historical Overview

In the Republican period, 1912–1949, there were over 350 New Zealanders living and working in China as long-stay residents.[1] They were protected as British subjects, in a China undergoing a complex and difficult transition following the fall of the Qing dynasty and imperial system, through toleration articles in key international treaties signed between competing empires of the imperial period. New Zealand missionaries were protected, and had their rights to exercise evangelisation and conversion through Article VIII of the treaty of 26 June 1858 which formally concluded the outcome of the second Opium War, and Article XIII of the treaty of 5 September 1902 after the suppression of the Boxer Rebellion. Extraterritorial jurisdiction in the 'Treaty ports' provided further cover and protection for foreign imperial subjects in major metropolitan centres of coastal and central China, offering a zone of residence and activity exempt from Chinese law, tax and norms.

The majority of the New Zealanders worked for three main Christian missions: the interdenominational China Inland Mission (CIM) founded and based in Britain, the Canton Villages Mission (CVM) of the New Zealand Presbyterian Church, and the Anglican New Zealand Church Missionary Society (CMS). This main New Zealand missionary effort was supplemented by evangelists working for Brethren, Roman Catholic (Columbans), and high-Church Anglican missions (Society for the Propagation of the Gospel).

Aside from missionaries, a number New Zealanders worked for the United Nations Relief and Rehabilitation Administration (UNRRA), the

---

[1] For data and quotations during the Republican period, see Matthew Dalzell, *New Zealanders in Republican China, 1912–49*, Auckland, New Zealand Asia Institute, 1994.

Friends Ambulance Unit (FAU, later termed the Friends Service Unit (FSU)), and for the Shandan Bailie School in Gansu Province. There were miscellaneous others, including telegraph workers in Fujian during the 1920s, and some whose limited historical traces suggest tales of intrigue and tragedy, such as a certain Harold Lancelot Beachey. Working for the Banque du Belge in Shanghai until a brutal incident in one of the seedier quarters of the city, Beachey was left without a nose and to eke out an existence playing piano in hotel bars behind a curtain lest his appearance disturb patrons. The New Zealand official presence, as a colony and later dominion of the British empire, was maintained through British diplomatic and consular missions, although there were rather limited and short-term attempts to establish and run New Zealand trade commissions in Tianjin and Shanghai.

In 1949, however, a new government was inaugurated in Beijing under the leadership of the Chinese Communist Party. The new administration enforced common left-wing charges of 'cultural aggression' or 'cultural imperialism' against missionaries and other foreigners. Virtually all, including the New Zealanders, were expelled by 1951, some following lengthy and disturbing imprisonment and interrogation, such as Annie James of the Canton Villages Mission.

What then had been the impact of almost forty years of New Zealand social contact with China? Many went with a clear 'transformative intent' in mind, based on firm assumptions of civilisational, cultural, and imperial superiority: the primary unevangelised Other on the planet needed them, "China's millions" (as the CIM magazine was called) were heathen and unmodern, and New Zealanders responded in droves, answering the 'call to China' with presence, evangelism, and works.

By the end of the period, there had certainly been some Christian witness, as noted by the incessant reports from hard-working missionaries such as James Huston Edgar, who by the late 1930s was reporting on delivery of bibles and tracts by the ton to the Tibetan peoples in the Sichuan marches. Conversions were fewer, although customarily were profiled strongly in mission literature, and the beginnings of an effort to indigenise the churches had shown early promise. Medical and educational works, favoured by the 'socialisation wing' missions for their demonstration effect, were more successful, but this often was seen to be a diversion from the missions' prime purposes of witness and/or conversion. Unsurprisingly, the debate on mission methods, which had started with the Jesuits, remained vigorously contested right through 1949 and beyond.

In rural Gansu, Rewi Alley, "a new and strange kind of missionary" according to a contemporary, K.M. Panikkar, and the team at the Shandan Bailie School provided a useful working model for secular 'cooperative education' in technical/vocational subjects and what might these days be called integrated rural development. The model was largely ignored in favour of Stalinist big-plant operations, however, as peace and reconstruction were overtaken by more ambitious and revolutionary policies of the Great Leap Forward. One can only speculate on the current economic and social conditions of central and western China had a variety of diffused, small-scale, integrated rural and industrial development taken hold in the 1940s.

Humanitarian relief was largely of marginal or mixed success during the civil war period, variously misdirected, misappropriated, insufficient, undermined by bureaucratic and factional interference, and sometimes simply lost or wasted. For all that, over the period of the foreign assistance lives were saved, wounded or diseased and disabled people rehabilitated, communities rebuilt, and the beginnings of social infrastructure put back in place. The much larger reconstruction effort would have to be sustained locally, or through socialist fraternal assistance, after the expulsions of 1949–50.

The impact on New Zealand was probably greater. Missionaries and relief and reconstruction workers alike had a deep-seated desire to publicise their achievements and thereby gain continued moral, human and financial support for their continuance. Publicity was undertaken mainly through voluminous and frequent writings from the field, circulated through family and church circles as well as published, through deputation or speaking tours in New Zealand on leave or furlough, and direct lobbying of political and community figures.

Their efforts and impact contributed significantly also to the establishment and outreach of a popular enterprise for assisting the poor overseas, as seen in the founding of the Council of Relief Service Organisations (CORSO). It can be said that principles, methods and structures of development assistance in New Zealand, especially in its civil society form from the 1940s, were a direct outgrowth of both the missionary and reconstruction efforts in China.

Precipitous Decline

In the 1950s-1960s, after the massive expulsion of foreigners, there were very few New Zealanders living and working in China. Rewi Alley is the most prominent example, both living there and undertaking a prodigious amount of writing, and some speaking tours. There were relatively few visitors from New Zealand. Visits were possible and made in spite of the lack of diplomatic recognition, but in those circumstances generally required hosting by 'parallel diplomatic' contact channels, such as through the New Zealand China Friendship Society (NZCFS) and its counterpart, the Chinese People's Association for Friendship with Foreign Countries (known by its Chinese contraction, Youxie). Other visitors included photographer Brian Brake, various writers interested in 'New China' such as Margaret Garland, those on union, fraternal Communist Party or workers' tours (Vic Wilcox of the NZCP was a frequent and high-profile visitor), and some remarkably persistent traders (such as Ron Howell and Victor Percival). During this period, there was however a relative information gap for New Zealanders – a common experience for 'western' observers.

New Frameworks, New Growth

In 1972, with the Joint Communiqué on Diplomatic Relations, the door opened once more.[2] The key difference from the Republican period was

---

[2] See John McKinnon, "Breaking the Mould: New Zealand's Relations with China", in B. Brown (ed), *New Zealand in World Affairs, 1972–1990*, Wellington, Victoria University Press, 1999.

that the instrument and agreement were concluded by two fully sovereign and empowered nations, dealing on a formal and equal basis, bilaterally, and increasingly from that point in multilateral contexts too. Frameworks for facilitating two-way flows of people became matters for mutual agreement and/or domestic policy, in accordance with the pursuit of national interest in the world, not a by-product of the nineteenth-century exercise of imperial power.

In addition to political and trade ties, which were assiduously cultivated, frameworks were put in place to foster people-to-people links, in particular the China Exchange Programme (CHEP) on the New Zealand side. This was a phase of active support for expanding relations, including official facilitation and funding of cultural diplomacy and popular links, which lasted until the early 1990s. Then, in 1994, the task of CHEP was taken over by the newly-formed Asia 2000 Foundation of New Zealand which continued these efforts from beyond official circles. The programme had supported the studies and exchange of dozens of New Zealand university students and teachers, and fostered a broad network of institutional, research and technical cooperation links. The links were many and varied, and expanding, but some way from being sustainable in themselves, as the Select Committee on Foreign Affairs and Defence noted in 1986 in its comprehensive review of the bilateral relationship.[3] The committee recommended a series of actions for the government of the day, all designed to build a strong and broad relationship, and inevitably involving appeals for greater resourcing and coordination to official efforts.

The 1990s saw the emergence of another trend, with the increasing 'normalisation' of contacts between the two countries, after the relatively brief hiatus in contacts following the suppression of demonstrations in Tiananmen Square. Across a spectrum of official and diplomatic effort, but also in people-to-people links, the relationship began to resemble others that New Zealand had with countries of a similar size, in both

---

[3] Select Committee on Foreign Affairs and Defence, *New Zealand and China*, Wellington, Government Printer, 1986.

economic and geopolitical heft. The New Zealand Government put increasing emphasis on technical frameworks and the creation of an 'enabling environment' for growth in the relationship beyond political and security ties.

In a sense, there was a waning *need* for the New Zealand Government to work at the official level to add depth and breadth to relationship, but also a concomitant change of focus towards what was defined as the core business of political, security and trade relations. Notably, this change in focus occurred at a time of redefining the central mission and strategic goals of most public sector agencies in New Zealand. In the bilateral relationship with China, with the enabling environment largely established, civil society and the private sector were free to engage to the extent they had interest, desire and capability to do so. By contrast, there was some support for one-off and high-profile events encouraging people-to-people or cultural ties at key moments in the relationship, such as the NZCHINA25 celebrations and conference, the Rewi Alley Centenary, and the 30 Years On efforts of 2002.

The New Zealand Government has limited resources to promote and encourage bilateral relationships, including the one with China. By my count there are roughly twenty-five equivalent full-time New Zealand officials working on the relationship in China and Wellington, along with occasional ministerial and senior official attention.[4] With resources so arrayed, it makes sense in terms of allocative efficiency to focus official time and effort on those aspects of the relationship that most require it.

---

4 Beijing (12 seconded), Shanghai (3 seconded), Hong Kong (several seconded staff from three departments, but none involved full-time with mainland China issues), Guangzhou (Trade NZ, 1), and Wellington (MFAT North Asia Division (3), NZAID (<1), Trade NZ (1), NZIS (1), Department of Prime Minister and Cabinet (1), and portions of time and attention from other departments (such as the Ministry of Agriculture and Forestry, Ministry of Education) and agencies (such as the Refugee Status Appeals Board).

How Many? Why?

In comparison with the Republican and pre-recognition periods, how many New Zealanders have lived and worked in China since 1972? If the numbers can be traced, are there broad conclusions to be reached on anything significant or notable about that presence?

By my estimates, there were perhaps only dozens of long-stay residents annually through 1970s and 1980s, mainly students and some traders and advisors. From mid-1990s, however, there were perhaps several hundred. As of 2002, there may be almost 1,000.[5] New Zealand tourists are also increasingly numerous, and exploring a wider range of sites and settings, largely due to the Chinese government's opening up more areas to foreign visitors, infrastructure improving (both hard, such as transport, accommodation and communications; and soft, such as tour operators, guides, and interpreters), a greater emphasis in official policy on the benefits of inbound tourism, and the relative cost-effectiveness of China compared with destinations in Australia, Europe, or North America.

New Zealand data on travel by its residents does not give a complete picture of main destinations. New Zealand authorities frequently only discover how many citizens are living or staying in a country, where they are and what they are doing, when there is a crisis, e. g. the 1989 evacuations following the suppression of the Tiananmen Square demonstrations.

Numbers aside, New Zealanders' reasons for living in China have clearly evolved since 1972. Although many still aim to travel to China to teach, train, or transfer skills and technology, and many living in China have a clear and vocal sense of 'what China really needs', many also go to learn. Students, researchers, exchange fellows, institute staff and others are studying various aspects of local culture and practice, from traditional Chinese medicine, to martial arts, to architecture, art and calligraphy, to silviculture and horticulture.

---

[5] Briefing paper of the New Zealand Ministry of Education, *China: New Zealand-China Education Relationship*, Wellington, April 2002.

Enabling Frameworks: Macro Level

The keys to growth, outlined above, are the expansion of frameworks concluded at a government-to-government level, the greater ease for New Zealanders to travel and live in China, and providing support for the mid-level and micro-level agreements sought and concluded by non-governmental agencies and organisations. These agreements include:

- 1972 Joint Communiqué: diplomats, officials;
- 1975 China Exchange Programme: teachers, students, advisers;
- 1989 Investment Promotion and Protection Agreement (15-year time horizon);
- 1993 three Education MOUs: exchanges, technical advice, and curriculum development (currently being updated);
- 1993 Air Services Agreement, and later amendments;
- 2000–01 MOUs for joint commissions on Forestry, Sanitary and Phytosanitary (SPS) issues, Agriculture;
- 2003 (draft) Consular Agreement.

Each agreement provided high-level support for increasing people-to-people contact and in many cases for long stay residency and work. It should be recalled that exchange agreements and trade facilitation, through transport, border access and quarantine standards recognition, all provide opportunities where none or fewer existed before. Trade represents the successful culmination of longer-term processes of market appraisal, establishing contacts, and making an investment in at least a medium-term relationship with the seller, buyer or intermediary. It needs significant effort on the ground, and building of trust and goodwill with clients, especially in the absence of fully supportive domestic legal frameworks to underpin transactions. Larger New Zealand companies and investors have recognised the need for properly-staffed diplomatic posts so better to foster the climate for deals and trade to flourish.

- Other than the frameworks above, lower-level commitments were also entered into by the two governments. One was for bilateral development assistance. Although not covered by a formal instrument such as an agreement, there was an understanding from the late 1970s onwards that New Zealand had particular areas of skill and advice to offer China, predominantly in agriculture, horticulture, and natural resource management, and later, through the 1990s and to a lesser extent, also in governance advice and trade-related capacity building.

Government-to-government agreements which have and will have a bearing in the growth of this relationship also include multilateral agreements such as the General Agreement on Trade in Services. With China having acceded to the World Trade Organisation, both the Uruguay Round terms and Doha Round outcomes should permit and promote a wider range of services trade and contacts in the tradable sector, e. g. education commitments could enhance provision of in-country supply by New Zealand educational institutions, providers, or individuals; banking and financial services could be covered by WTO rules rather than bilateral and case-by-case approvals.

Mid-Level Agreements

There are fewer New Zealand Government agreements at this level, although some departments may conclude arrangements if there is a particular technical reason and strong business case to do so. It is worth noting, however:

≈ Asia 2000 Foundation of New Zealand (quasi-governmental): provides Higher Education Exchange Programme (HEEP), other programmes, ten students per year in agreement with China Scholarships Council under the Ministry of Education;

≈ Local Authorities: sister city agreements and understandings, over twenty with China, of varying substance and vigour. Interestingly, these are seen as governmental and expressions of foreign policy by

China, since the central authorities have a more direct-line relationship with their municipal counterparts than in New Zealand. Sometimes irritants, such as city agreements with municipal authorities in Taiwan, require explanation in terms of the different relationship between central and municipal governments in New Zealand compared with similar Chinese institutions.

Sister-city agreements have potential to enhance people-to-people contacts, forming an overarching framework for specific initiatives of those localities, such as school and sports exchanges, and have links back into education marketing and provision, tourism and cultural exchange etc. Some focus on cultural links, others are comprehensive and have strong economic and business motivations.

But they require enthusiasm and maintenance of the relationships, which are often subject variously to personalities involved, local-body party interests and platforms, resources which are subject to changes in local priorities and preferences for spending ratepayers' money.

The New Zealand Government has supported sister-city relationships in policy and principle. Given the interests and resources of the local authority and community, it appears not to have felt the need to provide active assistance to these relationships. The most frequent contact and expression of support seems to have been at New Zealand sister cities conventions and the occasional function at a New Zealand mission in China for touring delegations.

Micro-Level Agreements

As brief illustrations, these include:

- ≈ City, agency or institution initiatives, e. g. agreement on a touring art exhibition;
- ≈ University, faculty, or departmental MOUs, ranging from specific and active to generic and moribund;
- ≈ Crown Research Institutes;

≈ Trade and investment contracts and undertakings in the private sector.

Where Next; and Why?

Frameworks are now largely in place, and are analogous to those reached with other countries with which New Zealand has broad and substantial relationships. They are characterised by being *bilateral*, *open*, *transparent*, and *reciprocal*, unlike the situation in the Republican period. There are few signs on the horizon that would suggest waning or sudden withdrawal of official support for increasing people-to-people contact in the medium term.

The key to the next phase is *demand* and, to a lesser extent, Chinese Government regulation. So, to come back to an earlier question, "Where are we on the growth curve?"

On the positive side, there are a number of factors which suggest there is considerable scope for further expansion:

≈ Strong and close bilateral political relations, and rapidly expanding economic and trade ties;

≈ Growth and increasing liberalisation of the Chinese economy and its integration with the global trading and financial system, seen for example in the quantum of trade, in membership of APEC, in WTO accession and participation in the Doha Round of negotiations, and willingness to engage in freer trade negotiations with groupings of near neighbours;

≈ An increasing and significant number of New Zealanders of Chinese origin or descent who have family, business or other ties in China, whom Manying Ip has described as increasingly "transnational" citizens;

≈ Little sign of any lessening of New Zealanders' desire to travel, live and work overseas;

≈ The persistence and seductive power of a number of attractive myths of China for New Zealanders, as a place of projected fantasies, of mystique and adventure, however bizarre and anachronistic they may be (and which can on occasion lead, once misinformation or ignorance has been tempered by experience, to equally bizarre and dystopian visions of China).

But there could be limits on New Zealanders' ability and motivation to travel to and live and work in China:

≈ Language and culture: there is still a long way to go before native English-speakers in New Zealanders have functional fluency and comfort in Chinese languages and the cultural setting. The current priority and resourcing for Mandarin language study at secondary level in New Zealand will be an ongoing constraint in this area (in 2001 only 1,767 New Zealand school students studied Chinese, compared with 19,981 for Japanese and 23,816 for French)[6];

≈ Information: no news or information on China is published which is of special and targeted interest to New Zealanders, no journalists or columnists live and report from there, and there is very little marketing from Chinese companies, save perhaps in the sector recruiting teachers, and some in-bound tour operators;

≈ Opportunities: the economy is complementary to New Zealand's, but many areas of New Zealand skill and comparative advantage are in *services*, which are subject to tighter regulation than goods trades in industrial or agricultural products. There are fewer opportunities therefore to teach, do research, polling or work in media, provide financial, legal, accounting or other professional advice, or to write software with robust protection of intellectual property. The latter items may change over time, however, as a product of convergence with multilateral rules and norms, such as through the WTO Doha round negotiations on services trades, and/or passage and implementation of domestic law and regulation;

---

[6] Ibid. At the tertiary level, relative numbers are closer.

- ≈ Competition: better options arise elsewhere for many people who may be deciding whether or where to work overseas, by way of language facility, work opportunity, and ease of transferring self and funds in and out, especially in a period of accelerating globalisation and flows of people, in which countries and companies compete for skills (the global economy and system of state interactions is a long way from free movement of labour in the world which a number of economists have pointed out would be an axiomatic good – so bilateral deals on migration still hold sway);

- ≈ Resident visa requirements: some job classes are excluded or relatively restrictive, e.g. for journalists; extension processes and requirements and business visas are often seen as relatively inconvenient and costly.

Prediction might be difficult but it is probably safe to say that with the frameworks in place, and demand for the experience of expatriate life and work in China increasing, we are looking at a medium-long term rising growth curve, with minor risks of short-term dips. Where would the next steps be in further growth? Working holidays and visa-free access are logical extensions, as is a comprehensive free-trade agreement, but all would face policy and political hurdles. In any case, the opportunities are there for New Zealanders to take up if they wish: many do. Some may even not come back. Could we have a New Zealand cohort of China-based transnationals in time? That would certainly be consistent with the reciprocity principle in bilateral relations.

The Bilateral Economic Relationship and the Regional Setting

Robert Scollay

Although the characteristics of the two economies are obviously very different, China and New Zealand have in common the fact that they have each been undergoing far-reaching economic reforms over broadly similar periods. In both economies reform has been associated with increasing openness to the outside world, with the opening of the Chinese economy being especially dramatic. It is therefore not surprising that there has been a sharp increase in trade linkages between the two countries over the same period.

China's economic reforms began in 1978, and the reform process since then can in general be characterised as one of gradual transition from a centrally-planned to a market economy, a process which has yet to be fully completed. The reform process began in the agricultural sector with the introduction of the Household Responsibility System. Successful results there were followed by extension of the reforms into the industrial sector through a succession of measures centred around the Contract Responsibility System. The introduction of the 'open door' policy reflected a decision gradually to open the Chinese economy to the outside world. Foreign investment was encouraged to flow initially into a limited number of Special Economic Zones (SEZs), selected in part for their remoteness from the centres of political power and segregated to a degree from the rest of the economy. After a slow start, the SEZs quickly gathered momentum and, in the early years of their expansion, accounted for a substantial part of the increase in China's trade with the outside world. Successful experimentation in the SEZs was followed by the rapid opening of additional centres to foreign investment, with the result that the impact of trade and foreign investment has steadily penetrated further and further into the Chinese economy. Parallel to these developments, foreign exchange and capital markets were gradually developed. China's entry into the WTO is expected to assist in the consolidation of reforms to date and to provide a stimulus for further reform.

In New Zealand, the momentum for economic reform began gathering pace in the late 1970s and early 1980s. Gradualism gave way to a decade of rapid and far-reaching economic reforms from 1984, since when reform efforts have been much more modest. The reforms saw the sweeping away of large areas of regulation and of the protective walls that had hitherto sought to determine the relationship of the New Zealand economy to the outside world, leading to the emergence of a largely deregulated economy with minimal trade barriers. Accompanying these developments, the exchange rate was floated, financial markets were liberalised, inflation and government fiscal deficits were brought under control in the interests of macroeconomic stability, and substantial elements of the previously generous provision of social protection were stripped away.

It is against this background of economic reform in both countries that the development of economic relations between China and New Zealand in the last thirty years must be considered.

China in the World Economy

As its opening to the outside world has progressed, China has quickly emerged as one of the world's largest economies. Its ranking depends on the measure used. Using official statistics, China's GDP ranks slightly behind that of the major European economies, as Figure 1 shows.[1] However, by using the method of purchasing power parity (where GDP is calculated using exchange rates adjusted so that they reflect they reflect the relative purchasing power of each currency in its home country), China's GDP already ranks second in the world, ahead of Japan as well as the major European economies, as can be seen from Figure 2.

An impressive feature of China's recent development has been its ability to maintain very high rates of economic growth, even when economies elsewhere in the world are undergoing severe crises and recessions. As Figure 3 shows, China's growth rate in the 1990s was consistently high by international standards, even if the average rate clearly declined. China's weight in the world economy, already impressive, seems certain to continue increasing.

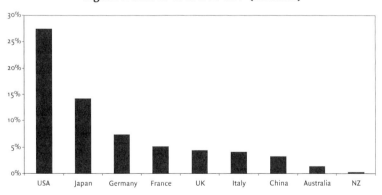

Figure 1: Shares of World GDP (nominal)

---

[1] Graphs in this paper have been drawn from statistics from the following sources: World Bank, *World Development Report 2001* (Figures 1,2), Asian Development Bank *Economic Indicators* (Figure 3), OECD Trade Statistics (Figure 4), IMF *Directions of Trade Statistics* (Figures 5–6), Statistics New Zealand Infos (Figures 7–9).

Figure 2: Shares of World GDP (PPP)

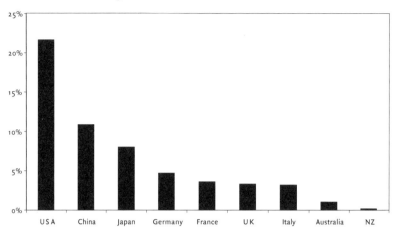

Figure 3: China's Economic Growth in the 1990s

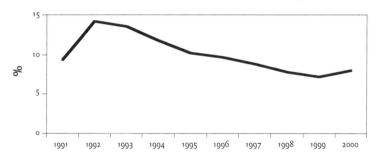

The progressive opening of the Chinese economy and its impressive growth performance has seen its share of world trade increase dramatically. As Figure 4 shows, China's share of world exports and imports was just over 1% at the beginning of the 1980s. By the end of the century these shares had risen to 5% and 4% respectively, and are certain to register further dramatic increases in the immediate future. As traders around the world are already well aware, China is now a major world market and a formidable competitor in the supply of a wide range of products.

THE BILATERAL ECONOMIC RELATIONSHIP AND THE REGIONAL SETTING

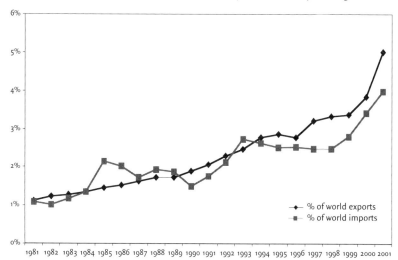

Figure 4: China's Share of World Exports and Imports 1981

China – New Zealand Trade

China's growing share of world trade has been mirrored by its growing share of New Zealand's trade, as Figure 5 illustrates. The share of imports grew slowly in the 1980s but then rose rapidly through the 1990s, from just over 1% of New Zealand's imports in 1990 to almost 7% in 2001. China's growing competitiveness as an exporter and the dramatic decrease in protection levels in New Zealand, especially for labour-intensive manufactured goods, were both clearly important factors behind this trend.

On the export side, the rise in China's share of New Zealand's exports was interrupted by a sharp fall at the time of the Tiananmen Square incident. The share then grew again but by 2001 had still not recovered to the level of the peak attained immediately before that incident in mid-1989.

New Zealand's share of China's trade, shown in Figure 6, is of course miniscule by comparison. The share of New Zealand in China's exports hovered around 0.1% (or one thousandth of the total) through the 1980s but then doubled in the 1990s. On the other hand there perhaps might be some concern on the New Zealand side at the clear declining trend in

Figure 5: China's Share of NZ Trade

Figure 6: NZ Share of China's Trade

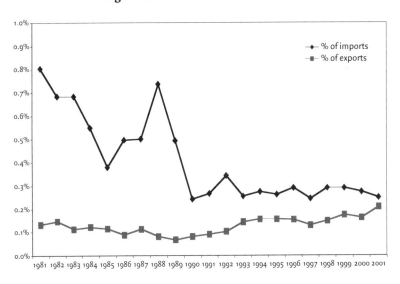

New Zealand's share of China's import market. Despite a rise in the mid-1980s, at the end of that decade New Zealand's market share fell precipitously. There was also a downward trend, though much less pronounced, in the 1990s.

New Zealand's exports to China are dominated by primary products

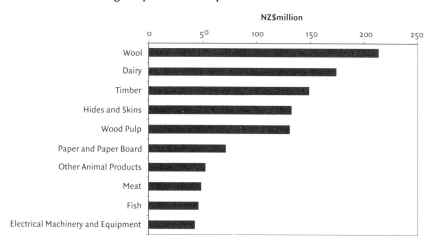

Figure 7: Main NZ Exports to China 2001

in both processed and unprocessed form. Figure 7 shows that primary products fill the first nine places in a list of New Zealand's ten main exports to China. Animal and wood products are predominant, with wool remaining the largest export, as it has been for many years, followed by dairy products and timber. China is a major factor in New Zealand's exports of a number of these products, particularly wool and wood pulp, for which China accounts for over 20% of total New Zealand exports. Its share of New Zealand's dairy and timber exports on the other hand is much lower.

Despite a very low share of China's overall import market, New Zealand exports do have a major share in the import market for some products. As Figure 8 shows this is especially the case for dairy products. New Zealand's share of China's dairy imports had reached almost 40% in 2000, after a dramatic rise in the late 1990s. The share of China's wool imports on the other hand declined through the 1990s.

New Zealand's imports from China are dominated by manufactured goods, especially apparel which is far and away the largest item. Most of New Zealand's main imports from China are traditional labour-intensive products such as apparel, footwear, toys and sports equipment. There are also significant imports of machinery.

Figure 8: Share of China Market for Main Export Products

Figure 9: Main NZ Imports from China

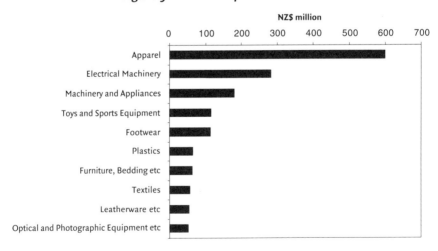

Implications of China in the WTO

After prolonged accession negotiations lasting 15 years, China entered the WTO in 2001. While this has been widely viewed as a dramatic development in the international trading system, the effects are likely to be gradual. China itself is likely to be the main beneficiary of its entry into the WTO, in two main ways.

On the export side, China will benefit from increased and more secure market access for its exports, especially in the textiles and clothing sector, where China stands to be a major beneficiary of the phasing out of the Multifibre Agreement under the WTO Agreement on Textiles and Clothing. As a result China's competitors will face intensified competition and the world market for textiles and clothing will be profoundly affected. New Zealand on the other hand may be relatively little affected, as it does not typically compete directly with China on international product markets. In particular, New Zealand is not a major exporter of textiles and clothing.

Internally, an important impact on China of WTO membership will be the 'locking in' of existing reforms through the implementation of China's accession commitments and its acceptance of WTO disciplines. Pressure for further reform will also emanate from the need to comply with accession commitments and WTO disciplines in areas such as services, state trading, customs valuation, intellectual property and standards and conformance.

In the medium to longer term China's trading partners will all benefit from a more transparent trading environment within China. The largest market-opening opportunities will arise in China's 'sensitive' manufacturing sectors, such as automobiles.

China's WTO commitments on agriculture are relatively limited. Accession does, however, mean that the existing level of barriers is 'locked in', thereby providing an insurance against possible future escalation of trade barriers, as has been seen in industrialising East Asian economies in the past. Agriculture has historically been a highly sensitive sector in China, being regarded as especially important for the maintenance of political stability. On the other hand China is also a significant exporter of some agricultural products. China thus has both defensive and offensive interests in international agricultural trade negotiations; and the stance that it adopts in the WTO negotiations will be watched with great interest.

Future Impact of the Relationship on New Zealand

China's continuing rapid economic growth and ongoing industrialisation mean that its demand for resource-based products is bound to keep growing. On the other hand the predominance of primary products in New Zealand's exports to China suggests the need for some attention to export diversification on the part of New Zealand.

On the import side, many of New Zealand's imports from China are already duty-free. Much of the potential impact on New Zealand industry from opening the New Zealand market to imports in these sectors has already occurred. The main potential for further impacts in future is in the textiles, clothing and footwear sector, which continues to enjoy substantial protection in New Zealand. Removal of that protection would place the sector under greatly increased competitive pressure from imports, a substantial proportion of which would be likely to come from China.

The Relationship in a Regional Setting

Since the late 1990s, as confidence in APEC has waned, there has been a rapid proliferation of proposals for new preferential trading arrangements in the Asia-Pacific region. Several agreements have already been concluded, and others are at various stages of negotiation, study or discussion. Some arrangements are bilateral, others are plurilateral, and there are also proposals that would lead to the creation of 'mega-blocs' on either side of the Pacific – the Free Trade Area of the Americas (FTAA) in the western hemisphere and an East Asian trade bloc in the western Pacific.

Northeast Asia, which accounts for over 20% of world GDP, holds the key to the establishment of any East Asia trading arrangement, which would necessarily have to include the three principal Northeast Asian economies: China, Japan and South Korea. There is a powerful economic logic favouring regional economic integration centred on these three economies, but equally there are formidable political obstacles in the way of any formal arrangement including these three countries, not least the difficult political relationship between China and Japan, the two regional economic superpowers. The mainland's relations with Taiwan also complicate the outlook significantly. China and Japan hold the keys to the form of regional economic integration that eventually emerges in East Asia.

The proposal for an East Asian trade bloc appeared to be gathering momentum, but more recently emphasis has shifted to an alternative model whereby separate arrangements might be negotiated between ASEAN and individual Northeast Asia economies. A proposal for a China-ASEAN free trade arrangement has moved surprisingly quickly into serious negotiations, and these negotiations appear to be moving quite rapidly. A proposal for a Japan-ASEAN arrangement has been moving rather more slowly, and would appear to favour a model involving a framework agreement with ASEAN as a whole, with free trade agreements being negotiated within that framework with individual ASEAN economies on a bilateral basis. An agreement has already been concluded by Japan with Singapore, and negotiations are now under way with Thailand. These 'ASEAN-plus one' arrangements are attractive to ASEAN as they offer the prospect of maintaining ASEAN in a central position in the trade arrangements of the region, despite the relatively small economic size of the ASEAN economies, which together account for no more than 2% of world GDP. The more negative implications of such arrangements are that they forgo the economic gains available from an arrangement embracing all three major Northeast Asian economies, while providing another channel through which China and Japan are likely to pursue their bilateral rivalry.

The risk to New Zealand is that there are obvious pressures to exclude it (and Australia) from most feasible East Asian trade agreement configurations. Exclusion would be very costly for New Zealand, and strenuous efforts will clearly be made to avoid this outcome. Allies will be needed among the East Asian economies. Among the three principal Northeast Asian economies China appears the least likely to oppose New Zealand (and Australian) participation on economic grounds, and the potential for China to act as an ally for New Zealand in this situation clearly merits further exploration.

New Zealand Business in China

Alastair MacCormick

In his novel *Soul Mountain*, the modern Chinese writer, Gao Xingjian, wrote of his experiences when visiting and studying the inscriptions on the tomb of the legendary emperor Yu who reigned in the 21st century BC. Gao surmised from the many ways of trying to read the inscriptions that history is a riddle or, amongst many other possibilities, a state of mind, analogy, or prediction; and he came to the conclusion: "Actually history can be read any way and that is a major discovery."[1]

This is not to suggest that the history of business connections with China can be read any way, although there are certainly some riddles. This paper is an effort to provide, at least in part, some explanation for the mixed experiences of doing business in China.

---

[1] Gao Xingjian, *Ling Shan* (1990). English translation as *Soul Mountain* by Mabel Lee, New York, Harper Collins, 2000.

New Zealand in China

Since the establishment of diplomatic relations between New Zealand and China thirty years ago, business connections have increased markedly. However, there were earlier pioneers such as Victor Percival of Kelvin Industries. It is fascinating to read the accounts[2] of his firm and the investments made in the decades before as well as after diplomatic relations were established, especially to see the difficulties and privations he encountered in setting up those first links in China.

This paper addresses the history of New Zealand investments in China over the last ten to fifteen years, although at some stage there is another story to be told about Chinese investment in this country. The general trade picture has been described elsewhere by Robert Scollay, and this paper focuses on listed companies, through their published reports, where the data is readily available.

The methodology is to look at a series of case studies in respect of New Zealand companies active in China. The context for this is the changing nature of the Chinese economy itself, since investment in China is at first sight attractive for foreign investors, including New Zealand-listed companies.

The Chinese Economy

The growing strength of the Chinese economy has been a major feature of the past two decades, and it is projected to continue unabated in the foreseeable future. An earlier New Zealand commentary on this can be found in the 1989 booklet *Meeting the East Asia Challenge: Trends Prospects and Policies* by Alan Bollard and others.[3] In that book they described the Chinese economy in terms of its enormous potential but

---

[2] See Victor Percival and Howard Scott, *China-New Zealand Trade: difficulties and successes as viewed from the perspective of the old China hand*, Auckland, Black Apple, 1986; and Howard Scott, *The strategic development of China – New Zealand Trade*, Auckland, Black Apple, 1988.

[3] A. Bollard, F. Holmes, D. Kersey and M.A.Thompson, Wellington, Victoria University Press for the Institute of Policy Studies, 1989.

were cautious about political stability and economic reform. They concluded that for the Chinese government, price reform would be a major challenge.

Leaping forward fourteen years since that book was written, we see that both political stability and economic reform have proceeded strongly, to the point where China has now joined the World Trade Organisation. The prospect is for further economic reforms which will mean that China's commercial environment becomes gradually more aligned to what foreign companies are accustomed to find in Western countries.

To elaborate on this, I am drawing on some statistical data on the Chinese economy from the Asian Development Bank about population and the labour force, prices, real income per capita and savings.[4] The population of China is very large and has been growing steadily over the last decades. Even though birth rates have declined, the population continues to increase; and this has been flowing through to a growing labour force. Around 18 million Chinese join the labour force each year; and while one has to net off those who are exiting the force, the point to note is that the entrants bring skills and levels of education far in excess

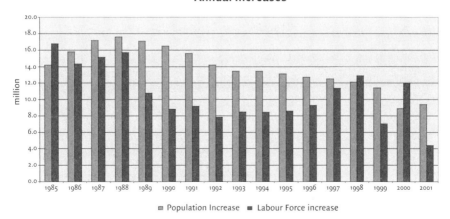

---

[4] www.adb.org: Key Indicators 2001 – Growth and Change in Asia and the Pacific

of those leaving. China will have a marked capacity to provide a cheaper and better-educated labour pool than many other economies for some years to come.

The other challenge that Bollard and his co-authors noted was price reform. Looking at the data on consumer prices, a period of considerable inflation from 1989 to 1996 has been followed by relative stability. During

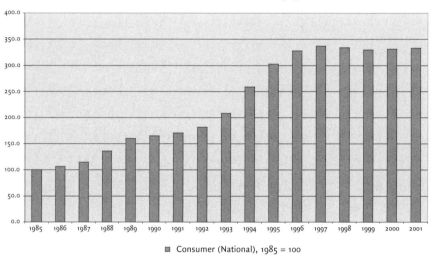

Consumer Price Index (National), 1985 = 100

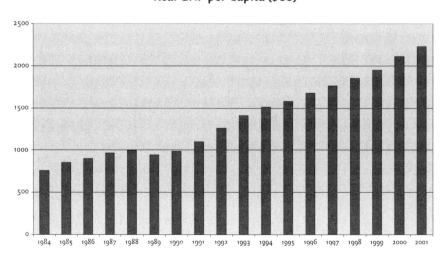

Real GNP per Capita ($US)

the period of inflation there was some pressure on the Chinese economy to devalue the RMB, but through all this interval China has been able to maintain the fixed relationship between the RMB and the US dollar.

Markets are increasingly functioning in China. However incumbent Chinese firms may have a competitive advantage stemming from state-provided capital that has been cheap. It is not clear that, when setting their prices, Chinese companies are required to obtain a rate of return from their revenue that will cover the cost of capital as well as direct costs.

Turning now to spending power, GNP per capita has trebled over the last decade, with steady increases occurring since 1991. However there are also very high savings rates, peaking at over 40%, so not all the increased income and spending power is flowing back to consumer spending.

The Lure of China

For foreign firms, China is on the face of it a marketer's dream economy. It has a massive and rising population, as well as rising incomes. It has some highly concentrated urban populations. So marketing planners see the opportunity to attract some of the increased spending power.

It is also a manufacturer's dream economy. There is an increasing and better-educated workforce that provides an ample labour supply at internationally cheap rates. At the same time there is massive investment to improve the transport and communications infrastructure. So it is not

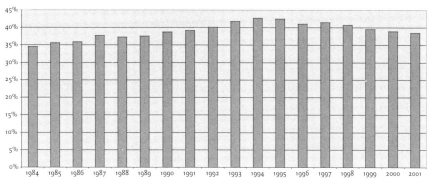

surprising that firms internationally are looking to investigate and enter the China market to establish a long-term position.

New Zealand Firms...
To turn now to the New Zealand firms that have made those investigations and decided to invest in China, the case studies which follow are of AFFCO, Fletcher Challenge, Lion Nathan and Richina Pacific. Sources include publicly-available corporate data and media reports.

...AFFCO
Late in 1998 AFFCO signed up to what was at that time the second largest New Zealand-China joint venture, to construct a modern meat processing plant in Chengdu, a city of around 11 million people in Sichuan Province. According to press reports, the project was thoroughly researched and confidently projected a rising demand for beef in China, which was consuming only 2.45kg per head of population. McDonalds of China enthusiastically attended the opening ceremony in May 2000.

Jinli, a land-owning company, was the first Chinese partner in the joint venture. The plant was built on land owned by Jinli, adjacent to a holiday camp. Jinli was also responsible for setting up and running a system for the supply of Golden Ox cattle crossed with European breeds such as Simmental and Hereford and procured from feedlots supplied by small farmers.

Equivalent in size to AFFCO's Feilding operation, its largest in New Zealand, the Chengdu plant was configured to process 100,000 head of beef and 400,000 goats annually. It was built to US Department of Agriculture standards. Wuliangye, the second of AFFCO's partners, had a network linked to 8000 restaurants and hotels, for the distribution of its famous white liquor and imported wines. Using this distribution network the product was to be targeted to top restaurants and hotels.

AFFCO held 30% of this joint venture, its contribution being made up of technology, plant management, its brand, cash and refurbished equipment from its recently-closed Waitara plant in Taranaki. AFFCO trained 13 Chinese supervisors in New Zealand. The then Chief Executive stated: "It gives us a local, tariff-free supply presence in a vast domestic market where the AFFCO brand already enjoys high recognition as a result of high quality exports from New Zealand."[5] AFFCO also saw the opportunity for New Zealand-sourced products to be sold alongside that produced in China, particularly renderings for which Mr Townshend quoted anticipated returns of $2500 a tonne instead of the current $70 in New Zealand.

Today AFFCO is no longer operating the Chengdu plant. On 18 May 2001 Executive Chairman Sam Lewis announced that a review had resulted in "the joint venture at the Wuliangye AFFCO Golden Ox plant in Chengdu, China, suspending operations at the plant until livestock procurement issues have been resolved."[6]

Supply problems had earlier been noted in a company publication. It would appear that the reliance on the Chinese internal markets for the supply of cattle for slaughter was misplaced. Location of the plant may also have been too great a distance from the feedlots; and this would have been a contributory factor.

. . . Fletcher Energy

Fletcher Energy was an early starter, being the foreign partner in the first foreign consortium to be granted a production sharing contract on the Chinese mainland. The concession was in the Dongting Basin in Central China. The 1992 Fletcher Energy Annual Report stated that exploration activities in Southeast Asia and China were active and innovative. Seismic surveys had started in China. By 1994 no commercial discoveries of oil or gas had been made; and by 1997 the joint venture was no longer mentioned.

---

[5] AFFCO Annual Report 2000, p. 13.

[6] Statement to shareholders, reported in *New Zealand Herald* ("Rough Time Cuts Affco Profits"), 19 May 2001.

... Fletcher Steel

In October 1994 Fletcher Challenge Industries announced it would acquire a 58% majority interest in a joint venture by investing $41 million in the expansion of an ironworks at Datong in Shanxi Province, about 400 km west of Beijing. The joint venture found the prices for pig iron were weak, but upgraded the plant to produce steel, for which it was expected the prices would be more attractive. After the first full year of operation it was reported that the venture had "provided a learning opportunity in a market with acknowledged potential". In 1997 the Annual Report indicated continuing problems: "Whilst technically the iron and steel plants are operating satisfactorily, financial performance is disappointing and a number of important management issues remain to be resolved with our partner." The 1998 report referred to trading difficulties associated with limited liquidity. The plant required a $10.1 million upgrade. "Overall however we have found operating conditions in this environment more demanding than anticipated and returns are currently unacceptable. The immediate priority is to improve operating cash flow."

By 1999 the joint venture came to an end. An operating loss of $11 million was reported. There was uncertainty about the viability of the business and Fletcher Challenge wrote off its total investment of $49 million.

... Lion Nathan

Lion took two years to evaluate investment opportunities in China before making its bold moves to invest in China. It looked at thirty possible joint venture opportunities and a number of locations before settling on the Yangtse (Changjiang) River Delta area with its population of 70 million.

Apart from the lure of the huge population, there was the potential for increased consumption of beer. Chinese were found to drink 14 litres a year, about half that of neighbouring Hong Kong and Taiwan consumers.

The first move was a 60% stake in an existing regional brewery located in the city of Wuxi. The Lion Nathan cash enabled the brewery to be modernised and its capacity doubled to 120 million litres a year. The local brand, Taihushui, was relaunched.

Encouraged by the early response to the revamped Taihushui brand, and driven to invest while plant and equipment could still be imported tax-free, in 1996 Lion Nathan committed to construct a 100% owned plant in a new economic development zone at Suzhou. The cost of the greenfields investment was $200 million. This brewing plant was state of the art and, with a capacity of 200 million litres a year, more than doubled the production capacity available to Lion in China. However, despite considerable marketing efforts concentrated on five major cities within easy reach of the plants, including Shanghai, sales have fallen short of the levels necessary to break even. The cumulative loss (before interest costs) is in excess of 540 million RMB or $138.8 million.[7]

RMB million	1997	1998	1999	2000	2001
Net revenue	143.2	272.8	254.9	206.8	224.5
EBITDA[8]	(47.0)	(144.8)	(142.1)	(123.8)	(83.8)

Lion Nathan has kept this investment going, despite the accumulated losses, waiting for the market to develop. Since the original investment was made Lion Nathan has had the support of a significant Japanese brewer, which took a major stake in Lion Nathan. This support, together with good profits from Australian and New Zealand operations, is allowing the brewer to take a long-term view. The last Annual Report hinted that alternative uses are being considered for the Suzhou plant.

With a large labour force of 870 employees, Lion is clearly positioned to take advantage of cheap labour rates. Nevertheless their investment in China is capital-intensive and will not move into profit until there is a major increase in throughput. A doubling of sales and maybe nearer a

---

[7] Annual Report 2001, p. 32.
[8] EBITDA – Earnings before interest, taxes, depreciation and allowances.

tripling could be required before Lion Nathan China will receive adequate returns on its investment.

Lion Nathan has found China a very competitive environment for beer, with many small plants still in existence and strong city and regional loyalties. It is also not the only foreign brewer to enter the market. Lion Nathan executives stress that "China is a long- term strategic move".

... Richina Pacific

Richina Pacific Ltd has evolved from the takeovers of the New Zealand companies Mainzeal and Mair Astley in the mid-1990s. Since then there have been two major investments by Richina in China: Blue Zoo Beijing and Shanghai Richina Leather (SRL).

Blue Zoo Beijing is an aquarium, opened in late 1997 by then Prime Minister Jim Bolger. It is situated in the east of Beijing adjacent to the Gong Ti Workers' Stadium (which is a joint venture partner). The site was made available by the Beijing municipality, and the Chinese partners take a small annual return from the venture. Management is vested entirely in Richina Pacific.

In its first year of operation, there were over one million visitors and it was relatively profitable. But in that same year, and despite earlier assurances from the Chinese authorities that it would be the only such aquarium for three years, two further aquaria were opened: one privately-owned and on a scale similar to Blue Zoo, but in the west of the city, and a second, much larger, aquarium, opened at the Beijing Zoo. This Beijing Zoo aquarium, being an investment of the state, appears not to be subject to the same commercial pressures to make a return as the private ventures.

Visitors to the Blue Zoo aquarium fall into several categories. Many are visitors to Beijing, including the strong domestic tourist market. In addition there are tourists from overseas, especially from Korea. Large numbers of schoolchildren visit each year, but their admission prices are not high.

After the first year, Blue Zoo has not been as profitable; and it made a small loss in 2001. At year-end 2001 Richina Pacific wrote down its investment by $18.6 million In the short run it is sustainable as the investment is cash-flow positive. There are some signs of recovery after numbers fell after the first year. Questions to be asked about the long-haul for this investment include the extent to which tourism will grow, aided by major events such as the 2008 Olympics, the extent to which Blue Zoo can gain a share of that market, and the extent to which the competitors may change their strategies away from the price wars of the past two years.

Shanghai Richina Leather (SRL) has been developing this leather manufacturing plant in the Baoshan district to the north-west of Shanghai for over five years. In a joint venture with the Shanghai Leather Corporation holding 5%, Richina has full management responsibility for the operation.

In the first years, significant losses were incurred, but more recently, sales have grown beyond the break-even level, and the plant is a profitable facility. Sales reached nearly $200 million in 2002 and are expected to double over the next two years, with relatively modest investment in plant and working capital.

Why does this particular investment have an excellent chance to continue to be profitable over the long haul? SRL is not dependent on the local market either for its supplies or for its customers. SRL has its manufacturing in China, but most of its material inputs are imported. Hides come from the United States, mainly from Texas, while the sheepskins are predominantly from New Zealand. Chemicals for the plant are imported from major global chemical manufacturers. The plant is reliant on China only for labour and utilities, such as power and water, and for transport.

On the output side, all the production is exported, although it may be converted to end product before it leaves China. The cow-hide leather is incorporated in shoes for major global brands such as Timberlands, Wolverine and Clarks, and sold into the US and other Western markets. The sheepskin leather is turned into garments for the US and other markets and are sold through large chains like K-Mart and Walmart. Recently, the SRL plant has diversified into producing upholstery leather for export.

The relative lack of dependence on the local markets is an important factor for SRL going forward.

Barriers to Success

In considering, from these case studies, what have been the barriers to success and why of all the cases only SRL appears to have profitable prospects in the short term, we find a number of factors in play. In some cases, there have been major difficulties in operating with the Chinese partners. This was especially true of the Fletcher steel joint venture and that of AFFCO where stock was not available for the slaughterhouse. It was also the case in the early days in SRL: only with the new agreement with the Chinese partner, which gave total management control to Richina Pacific, did the venture really begin to work.

On the output side, the only enterprises that have genuinely gone to market are the steel plant, where the sales never materialised in line with expectations, the breweries where sales never reached levels projected at the time the investments were made, and the aquarium where visitor numbers and the ticket prices have not reached levels forecast in the analysis undertaken prior to investment. What this suggests is that the Chinese consumer market is very tough to penetrate, especially with brands for which there is no ready recognition of the product on offer. Major world brands, such as Coca-Cola, McDonalds, GM cars, have established production facilities in China and have not withdrawn. It would be very interesting to know more about the extent to which they have sustained start-up losses in China.

The competition faced in the Chinese domestic market is very difficult, with stronger loyalty to domestic brands and local production than the international investors expected when doing their projections. Furthermore consumption patterns appear not to have followed expectations based on the experience in Western economies. Despite rising consumer spending power, it is possible that the Chinese consumer has a different set of spending priorities. For instance, Chinese are known to invest heavily in the education of their children, and this must absorb a considerable portion of their discretionary spending power.

It is also important to note the changing domestic economy. Now, with more Chinese owning their own homes, there is a greater propensity to invest in upgrading homes than before, when most dwellings were state-owned. So it is possible that spending on beer or other consumer items will not rise as rapidly in the immediate future in line with growing Chinese affluence.

On the other hand, where China has been used as a base for international production, it would appear that the investments may be successful. But of the cases above, only the tannery has promise for the short-term. The hypothesis is that this is occurring because it is not involved in the China market, either for its supplies or for its sales.

Among other factors, local and regional Chinese-owned plants may not have to show a return on their capital, either because they are not accountable for it or because it is already significantly depreciated. In the short to medium term, enterprises in this situation can more easily lower their prices to ward off competition from new entrants.

The commercial environment remains an uncertain one. Although the government has been introducing a commercial code, there is still not yet any high level of confidence in the application of this code in business or in the capacity of the legal system to enforce it. Furthermore, financing a business is still difficult in an environment where equity markets, such as the Shanghai Stock Exchange, are still under development. Foreign firms are not yet able to access such markets to raise equity. Chinese banks have no strong tradition of commercial finance, and foreign banks are wary about lending to businesses operating in the country because it remains difficult to secure the debt.

The conclusions to be drawn, therefore, are that domestic business opportunities in China are not quite as promising as investors originally anticipated. However, as the cases above demonstrate, investments in China targeted to export markets, and taking advantage of favourable manufacturing conditions there, seem to have the greater prospect of success. That said, while history might well be prediction and proof, as Gao Xingjian wrote, it would also be wise to temper categorical assertions about where New Zealand's business relations with China might be heading by recalling the great strides made in the thirty years reviewed in this series.

Relationship Dynamics and Strategic Calculus: A Chinese Perspective

Yongjin Zhang

Anniversaries are times for celebration as well as reflection. Three decades on since New Zealand recognised the People's Republic of China (PRC) on 22 December 1972, bilateral relations have matured and flourished in directions hardly anticipated or expected by those who opened the way for normalisation. By providing a Chinese perspective on the relationship, I hope to make this paper complementary to the others in this series.

One particular question I would like to address is what has driven the evolution of bilateral relations in the directions they have taken in the past thirty years. In looking for the answers, transformations of Chinese domestic politics and China's worldviews, in my view, provide major dynamics that underlie the direction and quality of this changing relationship. Understanding these shifts will surely help throw light on the future shape of this bilateral relationship in the next thirty years.

Recognition: A Long and Winding Road

As Michael Green rightly pointed out, geopolitical considerations prompted the Kirk government to recognise China in December 1972. This does not explain, however, why New Zealand had waited for more than twenty years to accept the international legitimacy of the PRC after its establishment in 1949. Why did New Zealand recognition come at that particular moment, not earlier or later? It is all the more puzzling because the early 1970s were probably the most chilling years of the Cultural Revolution. Domestic politics was in chaos, and even minimum order was yet to be restored in most parts of China. On the foreign policy front, China remained a revolutionary power deeply entrenched in its most radical, militant and uncompromising period in its support of revolutions around the world, and in advocating the total transformation of the existing international system. There were no fundamental changes in either China's domestic politics or its revolutionary outlook on international politics in the early 1970s.

New Zealand recognition needs to be situated in a much broader global strategic context. Of all the fundamental changes that underline the profound transformation of the global strategic settings in the early 1970s, one particularly worth mentioning is the changing philosophy of American foreign policy after the Nixon Administration came into the White House in 1969. This new philosophy, as Henry Kissinger later summarised succinctly, was that the United States would regard other ideological opposing great powers "in geopolitical rather than ideological terms".[1] That philosophy paved the way for the Sino-American rapprochement in 1972 and had profound implications for accommodating Revolutionary China into the international system.

For more than twenty years prior to 1972, the United States had pursued a policy of isolating Communist China as part of its global containment strategy against Communism. The Korean War not only affected New Zealand sentiment about China, which was branded by the

---

[1] Henry Kissinger, *White House Years*, Boston, Little, Brown & Co., 1979, p. 685.

United Nations as an aggressor. More importantly, perhaps, in the wake of the Korean War, "China and the United States confronted each other, at a distance, as implacable adversaries".[2] The American policies towards the PRC emerging out of the Korean War consisted of four pillars: non-recognition of the PRC, total support of Taiwan, opposing the seating of the PRC in the United Nations, and a total economic and strategic embargo against the PRC. These policies, aimed at isolating Communist China in the international community to the maximum extent possible, as well as at the outright denial of the international legitimacy of the PRC, remained largely intact until the early 1970s.

The United States also sought to persuade as well as compel its allies to make concerted efforts to implement American policies. Given the predominance of the United States in world politics and among its allies, it should cause little surprise that Canada was a 'reluctant adversary' of the PRC until 1970, and Australia's relations with China had to make the turn 'from foe to friendship' in the 1960s and the 1970s.[3] Both followed closely the American lead in their China policies. It should not be surprising either that the issue of the PRC's representation at the United Nations became a battlefront for its international legitimacy. The exclusion of Revolutionary China from inter-governmental organisations and multilateral international institutions was the result of a complex set of American policies and not a matter of choice for the PRC.

Like other close allies of the United States, such as Canada and Australia, New Zealand had largely followed the American lead in its

---

[2] Harry Harding, 'The Legacy of the Decade for Later Years: An American Perspective', in Harry Harding and Yuan Ming (eds.), *Sino-American Relations, 1945–1955 – A Joint Reassessment of a Critical Decade*, Wilmington, Scholarly Resources, 1989, pp. 311–12.

[3] See Paul Evans and Michael Frolic (eds.), *Reluctant Adversaries: Canada and the People's Republic of China, 1949–1970*, London, University of Toronto Press, 1991; and Edmund Fung and Colin Mackerras, *From Fear to Friendship: Australia's Policies towards the People's Republic of China – 1966–1982*, St. Lucia, Qld., University of Queensland Press, 1985.

China policies in this period. Throughout the 1950s and the 1960s, the recognition issue did come up from time to time in domestic political debates and was explicitly advocated in some Labour Party documents. Walter Nash as Prime Minister in 1958 toyed with the idea of recognising China.[4] The foreign affairs bureaucracy had to deal with the issue of China's representation at the United Nations on a yearly basis. Indeed, the issues of recognition and the representation of China at the United Nations had never been completely off the agenda of any New Zealand government throughout the period. In the end, however, the Cold War confrontation between the East and the West, the alliance politics particularly within ANZUS and New Zealand's own security interests in relation to the perceived Communist threat in the Pacific, conspired to withhold New Zealand's hand from recognition. At the United Nations, New Zealand co-sponsored a number of American-proposed resolutions, at the request of the United States, from the Important Question resolution to the dual representation resolution right up to the last vote designed to thwart the seating of the PRC.[5]

Indeed, given the strategic configuration of the international system and the prevailing power of the United States, the intransigence on the part of the United States in its China policy, and New Zealand dependence on the United States for its security guarantee, there was little opening for New Zealand to pursue a China policy directly contradicting that of the United States. Prime Minister Holland put this inhibition bluntly in a note to the Department of External Affairs in 1956.

---

[4] See, for example, Susie Ong, "Between Great Britain and the United States: New Zealand and the Recognition of China in the 1950s", in Yongjin Zhang (ed), *New Zealand and Asia – Perception, Identity and Engagement*, Auckland, Asia 2000 Foundation and New Zealand Asia Institute, 1999, pp. 91–2; and Keith Sinclair, *Walter Nash*, Auckland, Auckland University Press, 1976, p. 295.

[5] See John Scott, "Recognising China", in Malcolm McKinnon (ed), *New Zealand in World Affairs, Volume II 1957–1972*, Wellington, New Zealand Institute of International Affairs, 1991, pp. 227–52.

While conceding the rationale and need for recognising Beijing and seating it in the United Nations, Holland nevertheless advised that "we should not seek the displeasure of our friends [US] by doing something which would cause them great displeasure."[6] Only fundamental changes in American China policy, symbolised by Henry Kissinger's secret visit to China in July 1971 and the subsequent visit by Nixon to Beijing in February 1972, would open the possibility of New Zealand recognition.

As late as November 1972, after his election victory that month, the new Prime Minister, Norman Kirk, was indicating that recognition would only be considered in his second term.[7] But events soon took their own momentum. The final timing of New Zealand recognition seemed to be heavily influenced by the Australian schedule for establishing diplomatic relations with China. On 22 December 1972 New Zealand became the 88th country to recognise the PRC, one day after Australia.[8] It was scarcely coincidental that Prime Minister Kirk chose to elaborate on the broad outlines of foreign policy of his government on the same day recognition was announced – a decision strongly linked to New Zealand's agonising search for an independent foreign policy.[9]

This had been a period of almost total non-communication between the two states and two peoples. As late as 1972, the only official channel open for communication between Wellington and Beijing was at the United Nations in New York. Non-official economic and cultural exchanges were minimal. The New Zealand Government had no means to make any independent assessment of whatever was happening in

---

[6] Quoted in Susie Ong, "Between Great Britain and the United States: New Zealand and the Recognition of China in the 1950s", p. 92.

[7] See John Scott, "Recognising China", p. 249.

[8] For the first twenty years of the PRC, from October 1949 to the end of 1969, only a total of 51 countries recognised the PRC. For the three years from 1970 to 1972, however, a total of 38 countries recognised the PRC, including most of America's allies.

[9] Norman Kirk, *New Zealand in the World of the 1970s*, Wellington, Ministry of Foreign Affairs, 1972.

China. If Chinese knowledge about New Zealand was clouded by myth and ignorance, New Zealand's understanding of China as a revolutionary power and a Communist state, and the scare of a China threat so much influenced by the so-called domino theory, was also certainly marred by misperception, misinformation, and preconceived ideas.

Towards a Dynamic Relationship: The Three Decades
Three decades on, what is behind the development of this increasingly dynamic and thriving relationship? Relations between China and New Zealand have evolved from those dominated by simple and single-dimensional geopolitical considerations in the 1970s to ones characterised by a rich tapestry of intense political, economic, cultural, and social engagement between the two countries at the bilateral as well as the multilateral level. The domestic transformation of Chinese politics and economy, and its subsequent changing international outlook and foreign policy are arguably the most important explanatory variables for this rapidly-changing relationship. From the Chinese perspective and for analytical purposes, these three decades can be divided into three periods, each leading to a higher stage of evolution of the bilateral relations.

The first period ran from 1972 to the end of that decade, when the so-called strategic triangle featuring Beijing, Washington and Moscow dominated Chinese strategic thinking. Chinese foreign policy was guided by Chairman Mao's 'three worlds' theory. China's obsession with anti-Soviet hegemonism in its international diplomacy led China to adopt a united front strategy in countering the perceived Soviet expansionism worldwide. For two reasons, New Zealand (as well as Australia) was seen as a natural partner in the united front against Soviet expansionism, particularly in the Pacific. First, New Zealand shared China's concern about Soviet expansionism. Furthermore, as a close ally of the United States in the region, it shared a similar strategic outlook on the potential Soviet threat to regional peace and stability. The entrenchment of the Soviet Union in Southeast Asia in the late 1970s through its alliance relationship with, and naval bases in, Vietnam hardened such a perception. After the normalisation of Sino-American relations in 1978 and the Soviet invasion of Afghanistan in 1979, a tacit Sino-American strategic alignment emerged to counter the Soviet threat. Such geostrategic thinking and geopolitical considerations provided the foundation for Chinese policies towards New Zealand during the period.

Indeed, the subject was raised during Prime Minister Muldoon's key visit to Beijing and his meeting with Chairman Mao on 30 April 1976, just a few months before Mao's death. As Muldoon recalled, in this ten-to-fifteen minute meeting, Mao expressed his concern about the Soviet threat and at the same time showed his understanding of New Zealand concern about China's atmospheric tests of nuclear weapons.[10]

The second period spans most of the 1980s. The launch of economic reforms and opening at the end of 1978 started what was later called China's 'second revolution', which would fundamentally transform China's social and economic landscape. Domestically, the Chinese Communist Party began to reposition itself to take up this formidable challenge ahead. This entailed a re-evaluation of the Cultural Revolution and a reassessment of Mao's legacies. In spite of intense jostling for power at the top of the Chinese leadership, by the early 1980s this process was largely completed. By then, China had also clearly abandoned Mao's three worlds theory as a guide to its foreign policy. In 1982, a reorientation of Chinese foreign policy was publicly declared. China began to move towards an independent foreign policy aimed at opposing

---

[10] Robert Muldoon, *Muldoon*, Wellington, A.H. & A.W. Reed, 1977, pp. 128–9. More detailed and elaborate discussions about the shared concern about the Soviet expansionism were conducted between Muldoon and Hua Guofeng, the Chinese Premier. For a brief description of these discussions, and those of his second visit in 1980 when he was the first foreign leader to meet the new Premier Zhao Ziyang (a meeting attended by one of this book's editors), see Barry Gustafson, *His Way: A Biography of Robert Muldoon*, Auckland, Auckland University Press, 2000, pp. 226–9.

both the Soviet and the American hegemonism in international affairs. In Deng Xiaoping's formulation, this policy means that China would not play either the Soviet or American card in world politics. Nor would it allow others to play a China card. In 1985, this policy evolved further into an independent foreign policy of peace. Seeking a peaceful international environment for domestic economic reforms became the goal of Chinese foreign policy. China did not become a status quo power by this shift of foreign policy. It did, however, signal the end of China as a revolutionary power and its ready acceptance of the configuration of the existing international political and economic system. The 1980s became the first decade in which China sought close political and economic integration into the global international society.

The evolution of China's independent foreign policy of peace coincided with New Zealand's dramatic assertion of its independent foreign policy through its anti-nuclear policy, triggering off the ANZUS crisis in 1984–1985.[11] Such coincidence provided certain dynamics for the bilateral relations. First, China was pursuing a policy of a nuclear-free South Pacific and would sign the Treaty of Rarotonga in 1989. There was therefore shared mindedness on this issue. Secondly, and more importantly, the New Zealand government's refusal to allow the USS *Buchanan* to visit New Zealand on the ground that it might carry nuclear weapons was seen in Beijing as courageous foreign policy behaviour by a small state and a close ally of the United States in standing up against the American hegemony. Thirdly, the subsequent parting of New Zealand from the ANZUS alliance warranted a re-evaluation of New Zealand's strategic value in Chinese foreign policy, in particular towards the South Pacific.

The full implications of the political and economic changes in China in the 1980s for New Zealand-China relations can only be

---

[11] See Malcolm McKinnon, *Independence and Foreign Policy: New Zealand in the World since 1935*, Auckland, Auckland University Press, 1993, pp. 278–301.

scenario.[15] Given the broad strategic interests New Zealand shares in regional peace,stability and prosperity, and its track record in standing up to the American pressure, China sees New Zealand as one potential force in countering the overwhelming power of the United States in the region.

China is particularly encouraged by the stance that the New Zealand Government has taken on regional security issues concerning China. Both government and public manifested little enthusiasm for the 'China threat' chorus in the mid-1990s and advocated engagement rather than containment. New Zealand's early endorsement of China's WTO membership demonstrated that New Zealand has its own vision of how to manage China's rise as a regional power. As Prime Minister Clark points out in her address, included in this volume, the New Zealand Government does not see China as a threat to New Zealand's security.

Finally, New Zealand's geopolitical location and its identity as a developed nation are seen as affording it a strong influence and unique role in the South Pacific region. This is strengthened by New Zealand's historical relationships with the United Kingdom and with the South Pacific nations. Although China does not seem to have any substantive strategic ambition in the South Pacific, the region is an important theatre for the perpetual tussle between China and Taiwan for international recognition. That interest needs to be taken care of.

The Next Thirty Years

Three decades on, this bilateral relationship has a qualitatively different basis. It is based on accumulated knowledge and increasing mutual understanding between the two societies and two peoples, rather than myth and ignorance about each other. It is based on open acknowledgement of differences in values, beliefs and political systems, rather than suspicion and distrust. It is based on independent assessment of

---

[15] For the full implications of such a scenario for Australia, see Stuart Harris, *Will China Divide Australia and the United States?*, Sydney, Australian Centre for American Studies, 1998.

each other's national interests and how best to pursue those interests in the global and regional settings. It is a thriving bilateral relationship that both sides value highly and nurture diligently.

What about the next thirty years? It seems that both the direction and content of the relationship will be defined, even more than in the past three decades, by what happens in China domestically and by how the international system accommodates the rise of China. There may be surprises, twists and turns, but political, economic and social transformations in China will be profound. If the leadership changes unveiled at the 16th National Congress of the Chinese Communist Party assure a smooth historical transition to the next generation, China will become the second-largest economy in the world, the indisputable engine of growth in the Asia-Pacific under this generation of leadership, and will emerge as a regional power with substantial responsibility in the Asia-Pacific. These will be the two defining factors that shape the relationship between China and New Zealand in the forthcoming years.

Shaping Our Future Relationship

Rt. Hon. Helen Clark

Anniversaries are times to reflect on the past and look ahead to the future. In the thirty years since New Zealand and the People's Republic of China established diplomatic relations, both countries have changed, and China has changed especially dramatically. In this lecture series, speakers have reviewed the experience of those thirty years, and looked at various aspects of the relationship between China and New Zealand as they evolved during that period. Today I want to look ahead: to consider how some recent developments in the interaction between China and New Zealand may shape our relationship in the future.

Let me first recall, however, that the decision to establish diplomatic relations with China was one of the first major decisions of the Third Labour Government led by Norman Kirk. It was a decision taken for the good and proper reason that New Zealand's security and welfare could not be maintained or advanced in the absence of direct contact with the most populous country in the world, and one of the major powers of the Asia-Pacific region. In taking that decision Norman Kirk was mindful of the consequences for New Zealand's then existing relationship with Taiwan. The government ensured that relations of a non-political, non-diplomatic character with the people of Taiwan were safeguarded. New Zealand governments since then have honoured the commitments made to the People's Republic on the 'One China' policy at that time, and my government will continue to do so.

In looking at aspects of New Zealand's relations with China today, I want to consider how we interact as governments, how we interact as trade and investment partners, and how we interact as people. The China of 1972 had been isolated from much of the world, partly by choice, partly by circumstance, and partly by the actions of others. Its economy was inward-looking and its people had almost no exposure to the world beyond China. In all of these respects the picture today is almost unrecognisably different. China is an engaged, increasingly prosperous and confident member of the international community, and many of its people are travelling and studying all over the world, including here in New Zealand.

In 1985 and 1986, Parliament's Foreign Affairs and Defence Select Committee, which I chaired, undertook a study of New Zealand's relations with China. Already by the mid-1980s, New Zealand was hosting a large number of Chinese delegations from many sectors, especially eager to know more about the science and technology which had driven the development of advanced primary industries here. The relationship at that time, however, had a very formal character, compared to that of today. There were neither tourists nor private students from China; doing business there was difficult; and there was an absence of regional organisations in which China participated in an open manner with other nations. Relations could be characterised as friendly, but also distant.

Seventeen years on, New Zealand and China have come to know each other much better. At the government level, meetings are frequent, friendly, and where necessary candid. I visited China twice last year – once on a bilateral visit and the second time to attend the Shanghai APEC Leaders' Summit. China's successful hosting of APEC, together with its accession to the World Trade Organisation, and the decision of the

International Olympic Committee that it should host the 2008 Olympic Games, made 2001 a landmark year for its international standing and relationships. President Jiang Zemin paid a state visit to New Zealand when he attended APEC in Auckland in 1999; China reciprocally hosted Governor-General Sir Michael Hardie-Boys in late 2000. At Los Cabos, Mexico, in October, I again met President Jiang Zemin at the APEC Summit, and our respective foreign and trade ministers also met on that occasion. China's foreign minister has also visited New Zealand this year.

We note that a new generation of leaders is shortly to take office in Beijing. Our government looks forward to making their acquaintance and to welcoming them to New Zealand. While visits to one another's countries are always valuable, it is helpful and indeed essential that we also have other opportunities to meet and discuss issues of common concern, such as the dramatic developments relating to global security as well as economic issues. Our common participation in a great variety of regional and global gatherings, of which APEC and the ASEAN Regional Forum (ARF) are the most significant, is especially valuable for precisely those reasons. It is a marked contrast with the situation thirty years ago, when Chinese leaders rarely ventured outside their country, the visits of foreign leaders to China were a novelty, and China's participation in international organisations was constrained.

I said that our meetings are if necessary candid. There are issues on which we take different perspectives; indeed it would be surprising if there were not, given our very different histories. New Zealand ministers and officials will continue to raise issues related to the status of Tibet, religious freedom and other human rights, the application of capital punishment, and other such issues which are of concern to people in New Zealand. Naturally when such issues are raised, there is always an exchange of views. We believe, however, that the messages which New Zealand and other western nations convey are heard. Some recent developments in Tibet, for example, suggest that China is mindful of the concerns we and others hold.

China has now ratified the International Covenant on Economic,

Social and Cultural Rights. We urge China to ratify also the International Covenant on Civil and Political Rights. By their striving to uphold the human rights standards set out in the core international human rights treaties, I am hopeful that over the next thirty years in our relationship, divergent views on human rights will become less prominent in our dialogue, as China continues to deliver improved standards of living to all its people, and becomes more attuned to international standards and expectations. In the meantime, we will continue to have an open dialogue on these issues.

New Zealand does of course work closely with China in many areas. We have, for example, long-standing scientific co-operation. This year marks the fifteenth anniversary of the signing of the NZ/China Scientific and Technological Cooperation Agreement, which encourages the exchange of research ideas, equipment, and people between our two countries. Science, technology and innovation are vital to the sustained growth and development of both our economies. We look forward to welcoming both the Chinese Science Minister and his delegation to New Zealand when we host the 4th APEC Science Ministers meeting in March 2004.

As a permanent member of the Security Council and as one of the five major nuclear powers, China has distinct and equal responsibilities to bring about general and complete nuclear disarmament. This is a cause in which New Zealand has invested a great deal of time and effort. At the 2000 Non-Proliferation Treaty review conference, China, along with the other nuclear powers, made an unequivocal undertaking to accomplish the total elimination of its nuclear arsenal. We believe that a China determined to set the pace on nuclear disarmament would win plaudits from the rest of the world. China has taken the first key steps towards the end of nuclear testing: it has signed the Comprehensive Test Ban Treaty and ceased its own nuclear tests. We urge China to complete the process by ratifying the treaty. Such a step would offer leadership in the region and beyond. We do welcome the new regulations which China has put in place to control the export of missiles and chemical and biological agents.

Proliferation of weapons of mass destruction can only be curbed if all countries act individually and collectively against it. In that context we also urge China to exercise what influence it can to persuade its neighbour, the Democratic People's Republic of Korea, to give up any planning for a nuclear weapons programme and to honour the agreements it entered into with the international community in 1994. North Korea's pursuit of nuclear weapons does not enhance its security. Rather it sows doubt and uncertainty in the minds of its neighbours.

The need for co-operation against proliferation has never been more urgent as we work to combat international terrorism. As recent events have tragically demonstrated, terrorism knows no boundaries. All governments and all peoples are threatened by it, and all must co-operate to deal with it. China has demonstrated a strong commitment to the campaign against terrorism internationally, in supporting the UN Security Council resolutions after the attacks on the US, and regionally, through its contribution on the subject within the ASEAN Regional Forum.

A dialogue on defence is one of the more recent strands in New Zealand's relationship with China. This proceeds from our commitment to regional confidence building and has been advanced by the reciprocal appointment of defence attachés. China appears to takes the defence dialogue with New Zealand seriously, despite our differences in size and situation. New Zealand enjoys good access at the highest levels of the Chinese defence establishment. Good progress is being made in developing mutually beneficial defence ties, such as cooperation between our respective military educational institutes and the exchange of information through joint seminars and regular security dialogues. We believe there is potential for further co-operation in niche areas, such as logistics management, peacekeeping operation techniques, de-mining, language training, and personnel exchanges. While our security outlooks and defence priorities are very different, and while there is clearly a vast disparity in the relative sizes of our military establishments, there is ample scope for more interaction. It can also be deduced from this interaction and dialogue that our government does not see China as a threat to New Zealand's security.

Our economic relationship with China is also growing. China is New Zealand's fourth largest trading partner overall, and our sixth largest export market. The rate of growth of China as a market for New Zealand has consistently been above the average. Last year our exports to China increased by over $400 million, which is equivalent to adding another Singapore to our export markets. Furthermore, our exports to China have been growing faster than the average growth in exports to China from other countries. We are certainly getting our fair share of one of the world's fastest growing economies.

The lure of the China market has attracted generations of entrepreneurs and business people, and it has not always lived up to expectations. It is worth noting that South Korea, a smaller absolute market than China, takes more of our exports and provides more tourists to New Zealand than China. That tells us both what the potential of China is, and also that we have a long way to go to maximise our potential for trade with China. If we look thirty years ahead, at the current rate of growth in trade, China will rank in the top tier of our markets, alongside Japan, Australia and the United States. It is because of that potential that the recent government economic forum designated China as one of three major markets for a more co-ordinated private-public sector effort. Fonterra and Carter Holt Harvey, two of the largest traders into China from New Zealand, have agreed to lead this work.

China's importance in the global economy is growing steadily and it is now the sixth-largest economy in the world, and recently has moved up to become the world's fifth largest trading nation. As a developing country, China's growth rate is much steeper than those of the world's major developed economies. That was particularly evident last year when many of the world's developed economies were struggling. It also has to be much steeper than that of others if China is to keep abreast of the massive amounts of economic adjustment which are being required of its people as it integrates with the world economy.

China's voice will increasingly be heard in the councils of the global economy, especially given its entry into the World Trade Organisation.

New Zealand was an early supporter of China's entry, and we were also the first Western country in the WTO to complete accession negotiations with China, in August 1997. China's accession has improved our access to its market, in particular in respect of wool, which is our largest single export there. But there are broader implications too. Having forsworn subsidies on its agricultural exports, and having opened up its domestic agricultural market to international competition, China will also – we hope and expect – be a voice of reason in this central challenge for the world's trade negotiators.

The impact of China's economic prosperity and openness is being felt regionally. ASEAN and China have recently agreed on a programme to create a free trade area within ten years. This would rank as the largest free trade zone in the world in terms of population. New Zealand welcomes steps being taken to liberalise trade and investment, provided that they comply with the principles and intent of the WTO trading regime, and do not have the effect of creating barriers to trade with third countries. Again we see China, with its huge market and huge productive capacity, as potentially a new global anchor of more open trade.

Underpinning the contacts between governments and businesses is the presence of people from our respective countries in the other. New Zealanders can be found all over China, as students, as teachers, running small businesses from a backpackers' hostel in Lhasa to a fitness centre in Beijing, and even helping restore the fortunes of one of the largest clothing companies in China. About 65,000 China visitors come to New Zealand each year, making China our fasting growing tourism market. There are about 40,000 tourists visiting China from New Zealand each year – a number that I also expect will climb.

Given the importance of China to New Zealand and given some of the crass populism expressed about the presence of Asians in New Zealand, it is worth noting the long links between China and our country. In the second half of the nineteenth century the world saw the first outpouring of people from China. They were economic migrants, driven to seek their fortunes in other lands, especially in the gold rich lands of the Pacific rim. Indeed some of my forebears came to New Zealand for the same reason. The reaction of the lands to which the Chinese came, however, was not as welcoming as it was to Europeans. Earlier this year I acknowledged publicly that New Zealand in the late nineteenth century and early decades of the twentieth century discriminated against Chinese migrants unfairly, and I offered a formal apology for that. It was an appropriate and overdue recognition that the state had behaved badly.

For much of the twentieth century China was either too poor, or too much the victim of external aggression or internal conflict in earlier decades, to have much of an impact on the rest of the world. Poverty and politics prevented Chinese people from leaving China. That has all changed. China is still a developing country, but the standards of living of many of its people have improved immeasurably since the policy of reform and opening up was adopted in 1978. Many New Zealand visitors to China, and I count myself amongst them, are amazed by what they see in Shanghai and Beijing, operating as they often are with images of China which are ten, if not twenty, years out of date. Even people who have been absent from China for a much shorter period are startled by the rapidity of change. Not all of China is changing at the same rate or to the same degree, and there are growing inequities, between city and countryside, coast and interior, and sunset and sunrise industries. But China's membership of the WTO is a strong signal that China remains committed to the path of integration and interaction with the world. Even with uneven growth, there is still a substantial group of people, perhaps as many as 100 million, who have attained a "comfortably off" standard of living. That almost equates to the total population of Japan.

It is representatives of that group whom we are increasingly seeing in New Zealand, as tourists, students, members of official delegations, and migrants. They are skilled, able, and entrepreneurial. They are keen to learn English: indeed that is often why they come to New Zealand in the first place. They appreciate the stability of our society, they enjoy the clean and unspoilt natural scenery, and they are stunned by the low population density. The surge in numbers of these people is very recent. It was only in 1997 that we relaxed the criteria for the admission of

Chinese students to New Zealand. It was only in 1999 that China designated New Zealand and Australia as countries to which Chinese citizens could travel as tourists, a status not yet shared by many other western countries. We now have about 20,000 Chinese students in New Zealand. Last year New Zealand received 65,000 short-term visitors from China, more than double the number which came just two years ago. If the current rate of growth were sustained, we would be receiving half a million Chinese visitors by 2010.

This is not an entirely new experience for New Zealand. Something similar happened over slower time with Japan, and happened more recently, and with ups and downs, with Korea. The growth in the Chinese presence in New Zealand seems likely to be as quick as Korea's, as durable as Japan's, and larger than either. From time to time, however, the visibility of Asian migrants and short term visitors in New Zealand is the focus of political debate, and we seem to be in such a period again.

With respect to migration, it is worth making the point that with the significant exception of the first Maori, all people who have come to this country have found other people here before them. The process of adjustment which is required by new immigrant and old settler has been repeated generation after generation: it is part of what makes New Zealand the country it is. New Zealand and New Zealanders change, but much more change and much more adjustment are required on the part of the immigrant. This is a country which has welcomed migrants for skills, capital, and the new ideas they bring. They also bring a welcome diversity to our culture, and they add new strands to the fabric of our nation.

There can of course be short-term pressure points. For example, the numbers of Chinese students have expanded so rapidly in recent years that we are probably close to capacity in some cities and at some levels within the sector. If as sometimes happens, classes in business management are being taught in Chinese, then the overall value of the experience those Chinese students are gaining in New Zealand is reduced. There will be an optimal rate for absorbing large numbers of overseas students in total and from any single market. Our schools appear to be aware of when they have reached the optimal threshold, and they adjust their entry procedures accordingly. Responsible practice across the sector in all areas is essential if we are to maintain our international reputation and credibility. We cannot afford to have Chinese students arriving at a language school, for example, with the expectation (even if misplaced) that this will then automatically secure them a place in a tertiary institution.

We have made several substantive changes to our international education policies over the last twelve months to address this kind of issue and maintain the quality of education and pastoral care services which New Zealand provides. There will no doubt be more changes to come as the sector continues to evolve. In future we are also likely to see a greater move towards New Zealand institutions delivering courses to foreign students in their own countries, including China, to relieve the pressures on our own education system.

The presence of these students in New Zealand, however, is an investment in our future relationship with China. Most of them will return to their own country with, we sincerely hope, a positive impression of the country in which they spent some of their formative years. Already, returned students are playing significant roles in the New Zealand economic presence in China, whether in businesses on their own, or as the employees of others. They are a very large asset for us, with links all over China.

Tourists are more transient visitors, but they nonetheless can play a very significant role in our economy and society. They are generally attracted by what is different from their home countries, but, in the way of the world, they still expect to find home comforts. For tourists from China this can be as simple as finding a decent Chinese meal or being reassured with signs in Chinese. Some decades ago our tourism industry adjusted to the increase in tourists from Japan. The process will be similar with tourists from China, but the numbers may end up being larger, and the rate of growth steeper. I would certainly expect that thirty years out Chinese tourists will be a fixture in our tourist destinations, and that they will be spending at much the same rate as tourists from developed countries. Again, as with the numbers of students, care will have to be taken to see that New Zealand does not build up over-dependence on the sizeable Chinese market.

The last few years have seen, I believe, the beginning of a new era in our relations with the world's most populous country. There are two distinct but related changes: China is becoming a more significant voice in world affairs; and it is becoming a larger presence in our economy and society. These two developments are related because both rest on the fact that China is becoming a wealthier, more open, and self-assured society. Provided China continues with its current course of integration with the world – and I see no indication that it will not – then these trends will continue. New Zealand has every reason to welcome the increased prosperity of the Chinese people. We already have an excellent relationship with China. We can build on that to ensure that we share in China's future, and in the future of its talented people.

13 November 2002

Following her address, the Prime Minister responded to a number of questions from the audience. She acknowledged the presence of Hon Jenny Shipley, her predecessor in office, and her work – along with that of previous Prime Ministers – in promoting and developing relations with the People's Republic of China.

After the first question, about the impact of remarks by Hon Winston Peters, the leader of New Zealand First Party, about her government's policies on immigration and migrants – to which the Prime Minister indicated her government had never changed policies on the basis of his remarks – she was asked whether, with the growth in migrants and Asian population, especially Chinese, she thought that in 20 years' time there would be more Chinese MPs in Parliament.

Prime Minister: It is obviously desirable that the New Zealand Parliament represents the diversity of the New Zealand population. And I applaud the fact that Pansy Wong is now a second-term MP, as I applaud Ashraf Choudhary as the first MP from the Indian sub-continent, just as we have applauded the presence of the Pacific Island Members of Parliament. As the New Zealand population changes, so will the representation in parliament change. I think MMP has made it rather easier, because it has enabled parties to look at the overall composition of their list and give regard to the need for broad representation. So, inevitably, there will be more Asian Members of Parliament.

Emeritus Professor Nicholas Tarling recalled the populism around the stated economic benefits to New Zealand of the growing international student numbers. He asked for comment from the Prime Minister about what New Zealand could in fact learn from the students here and suggested that some of these benefits needed to be made more apparent.

Prime Minister: That might indeed be the occasion for another lecture! [But] as you have quite rightly stressed, there are two sides to it, or even multidimensional sides.

As I have constantly said, New Zealand's reputation must be staked on being a tolerant, accepting and welcoming society of all who live within that society. I've also acknowledged the huge economic benefits for New Zealand's having proportions of the population drawn from a wide range of countries with the ability to connect back in there. You have picked up the point I made about students from China having gone back home. It's not just that they have gone back home. It's that if they go back home and talk positively about New Zealand, how valuable that is to us as a small country that struggles to get recognition in a pretty crowded world.

You are right about what skills or values the new migrants bring to New Zealand. That makes us a more interesting place intrinsically to be. The efforts of organisations like the Asia 2000 Foundation reinforces that for us – such as with their lantern festival in Albert Park. And when I look back, comparing Auckland today to 1963, when I was a 13-year old in boarding school – it is a much more interesting, dynamic, cosmopolitan place to live in. And immigration has been a part of it.

The Prime Minister was invited to comment on the role of China in the growth of free trade arrangements in the region, including ASEAN, and how this might impact on New Zealand.

Prime Minister: This is about the overall issue of trading blocs none of which New Zealand is part. I do have a concern that there is a trend to develop a range of preferential arrangements none of which we are part. We are an export-oriented economy. When we see China and ASEAN doing a deal, and we can't do one with ASEAN – as New Zealand and Australia have been trying; when China, Korea and Japan sign an economic cooperation agreement; when we see President Bush at APEC inviting all the ASEAN leaders and offer to negotiate free trade arrangements with every one of them; when we see the United States offering to do a trade agreement with the Americas; when we see the same offer made to all the southern African economic community; when we know the preferential arrangements the EU has for itself; where does New Zealand fit in?

Trading for us is a matter of life and death, we are a small economy and geographically isolated. I think that the relationship with China may well be positive for us in that link to ASEAN. It's a point we can make in our representations to China, to keep the economic dialogue as broad as possible, and to encourage others to broaden theirs as well.

Afterword:
The Next Thirty Years

Paul Clark

Establishing diplomatic relations with Beijing thirty years ago took a leap of faith. Securing the New Zealand-China relationship and growing it over the next thirty years require an effort of conviction. In such a relationship of imbalance, most of this effort must come from New Zealand. At the next thirty year milestone, the China link will quite probably be this country's most important bilateral relationship (with the exception of trans-Tasman ties). Thirty years ago officials drove diplomatic recognition. Now New Zealanders at all levels need to be encouraged and enabled to take ownership of our China ties. The rewards will be enormous.

In 1972 person-to-person relations between New Zealand and China were of a highly marginal nature. I remember in July 1973 on the riverfront in Shanghai being asked, in English, if I knew 'Wei'erkekesi'. Victor G Wilcox (1912–1989) was the second most well-known New Zealander in China. As secretary-general of the NZ Communist Party, he was virtually unknown in New Zealand. China's most well-known New Zealander in the 1970s and 1980s was, of course, Rewi Alley, a professional 'friend of China'. A small coterie of 'peace activists' had kept the Alley flame alive in New Zealand after the establishment of the People's Republic in 1949. Alley's position in Beijing opened doors for New Zealand diplomats and helped them keep perspective on political developments in China. The early popular exchanges moved beyond diplomats to include students. The first three New Zealand exchange students arrived in Beijing in mid-October 1974 and entered the Peking Languages Institute. Chinese students started English-language classes at Victoria University of Wellington at about the same time.

When the Kirk government took that leap of faith in 1972, trade was not a major motivation, as Bryce Harland noted, though the possibilities obviously appealed. Even in 2003 many New Zealanders seem to think automatically of trade when relations with the countries of Asia are mentioned. Cultural, political and more personal ties with Asia have occupied a secondary position in public consciousness. This will change in the next thirty years.

With China, these perceptions are changing already, particularly in Auckland, where the strongest Chinese presence is asserting itself. Export education has attracted large numbers of Chinese students to undertake English-language study in New Zealand. By 2003 about a fifth of Auckland's central business district office and accommodation space was given over to such educational ventures and their students. A high proportion of such students were from China: here for short-term training or starting on a staircase of study extending to postgraduate degrees.

After thirty years personal connections between the two nations have widened and deepened. New Zealanders living in Beijing number in the hundreds: they study, teach, consult and serve in a range of arenas, bilateral and international. Visits by tourists and delegations cover a gamut of professions and regions. Sister city links and international consumer franchises being served by professionals from both countries were barely dreamt of thirty years ago.

Immigration of permanent residents from China and the Chinese diaspora has brought a personal dimension to the relationship.

Sojourners here for education are often difficult to distinguish from immigrants who are moving from permanent residence visas to naturalised citizenship. For many New Zealanders, Chinese immigrants are indistinguishable from Korean permanent residents or Japanese visitors. Unfamiliarity can breed contempt and alarm at the changing face of Auckland in particular, where most immigrants from Asian countries are making their homes and the largest proportion of students from Asia are attending classes. At the turn of the millennium, there are some small signs of hope that cultural tensions can be ameliorated and the social explosions some commentators feared avoided. Familiarity, at least among the school-age populations, is encouraging acceptance of the changing face of New Zealand society. Older citizens are more slow in their acknowledgement of change and open to political exploitation of their disquiet. Meanwhile Beijing is keeping a watching brief on developments: targeting of Chinese tourists by thieves has been reported in Chinese newspapers and commented upon by Foreign Ministry spokespersons.

The economies and societies of both countries have been transformed in the first thirty years of their diplomatic relations. We can assume that both nations will continue to change in the next thirty years. Given the huge size of their country, Chinese leaders will always be obsessed with internal matters, be they economic or political. But having entered the WTO and becoming a more normal and accepted member of the community of nations, China, it is reasonable to assume, will be more active in world and regional affairs than it has been in the last thirty years. This will be disruptive of long-standing assumptions and existing security and other arrangements built to contain a less developed, more isolated China. Assumptions that economic prosperity in China will lead naturally to a more open, democratic political system without a single ruling party may also be misplaced. In this dimension too, the size of China will be an important factor in determining what political arrangements emerge for its governance.

Notwithstanding its size and relative geographical isolation, New Zealand has always found ways to punch above its weight in world affairs. In much of the twentieth century, we discovered the means to do this in alliances with imperial powers, proving our value with our young men's blood by joining any war that involved our imperial patrons. By the end of the century a kind of Scandinavian position, associated with the Western alliance but capable of standing aside and serving as an honest broker, had been identified as a more effective way of securing a voice in international affairs.

History provides one way of predicting the future. Since Chinese first arrived in New Zealand more than two hundred years ago, the relationship between the two places has been set in a broader Asia-Pacific context. Sealers and whalers in the late eighteenth century were in part providing a Chinese market. Western missionaries came to New Zealand and went to China. By the end of the nineteenth century, missionaries home-grown in New Zealand were working in southern China. The first Chinese settlers in New Zealand were part of a Pacific rim series of gold rushes: California, Victoria, New Zealand, the Yukon. The post-World War II positions of Japan, Korea and China were of course products of the broader Asia-Pacific context. Waves of twentieth-century settlers and short-term sojourners, like the current rush of Chinese students, were part of wider mobility across the Pacific. The New Zealand experience with China and Chinese has always fitted a broader pattern and will continue to do so into the future.

In the future one thing will not change: our China relationship will remain an imbalanced and somewhat unnatural one. Despite the growing presence of Chinese in New Zealand, to most New Zealanders China will continue to seem a more foreign place than, say, Britain or Australia. The imbalance in size means that New Zealand need not figure much in China's view of the world or even the region. We must work on being noticed and even important in China.

New Zealand must accordingly devote considerable attention to working on the relationship with its biggest neighbour to the north. Our international stance, as a member of the Western alliance but not entirely subsumed under an American imperium, puts us in a special position in international diplomacy. We can prove a useful contact or go-between in relations among larger, more self-conscious powers. In late 1999 the Chinese and American presidents were able to meet in Auckland after months of tensions between Beijing and Washington. Our hosting of the annual APEC meeting provided the context for this encounter. But it points the way in which, in a less public fashion as well as in open diplomacy, New Zealand can be a useful regional player and assist our huge neighbours.

As something of an economic, social and environmental laboratory, New Zealand has the advantage of its relatively small size and geographical location. Women gained the vote first in this country; the welfare state became an early reality here; and we have been at the forefront in trade liberalisation and the dismantling of agricultural subsidies. This country can continue to offer its experience in these areas to other nations, including China.

But the relationship between our two countries requires work. The first thirty years have been the easy part. With China developing as the major power in Asia and the western Pacific, our success in building this relationship in the next thirty years is central to New Zealand's future as an independent and prosperous nation. This is not just a matter of the bilateral relationship. China will loom so large in world affairs by mid-century that a failure to seize the moment now to build the relationship will mean opportunities lost.

New Zealanders in all walks of life, in all parts of the country and of all cultural backgrounds need to become China-conscious at work and at home. China probably cannot take over the position that American popular culture occupies in all our lives. But making room for a Chinese presence in our world-views, and getting ahead of the need to do this as China grows more prosperous and powerful, will pay enormous dividends in a country that the world can easily ignore.

A focused effort by New Zealand business, government and communities to build the China relationship could help determine the future of our connections with China and ensure we continue to have a relatively high profile in that country. Ways to expose New Zealanders in all professions and sectors to counterparts in China, means to exchange best practice in education, local government, environmental protection and a host of other fields, activities to increase understanding of each other's histories, cultures and attitudes all require concerted organisation and funding. Incorporation of Chinese history, culture, geography and language in the school curricula at primary and secondary levels is imperative.

A New Zealand-China Foundation could positively shape the ways in which relations between our two countries develop over the next thirty years and beyond. With sufficient resources from the public and private sectors, a foundation could be the focal point for large-scale exchanges between the two countries. One hundred primary school teachers travelling in each direction for several-month assignments at counterpart schools would make a small, but significant contribution to China's English-language and cultural learning needs. In New Zealand Chinese teachers could bring the reality of a modern, prosperous China home to all regions. Touring drama and dance companies could raise New Zealand's creative profile. Chinese and New Zealand imaginations could create extraordinary results: imagine a shared wearable arts festival in Auckland and Shanghai. Chinese conservationists have been saving the giant panda, New Zealanders are saving the kakapo: they could learn further from each other. Town planners, building inspectors and accountants, to identify just three professional fields, could also exchange experiences and broaden horizons.

New Zealand's future prosperity and international relevance could depend on the success of such a venture. The leap of faith in 1972 produced a healthy relationship. An effort of conviction is now required to grow this relationship that will be so central in our future.

NEW ZEALAND ASIA INSTITUTE

Details of Institute activities and publications, including its regular newsletter, *Asia Info*, can be found at www.auckland.ac.nz or by email to nzai@auckland.ac.nz